ZENTANGLE®
Step by Step

Hannah
Geddes

Acknowledgments

The Zentangle® method was created by Rick Roberts and Maria Thomas.

"Zentangle"®, the Zentangle logo, "Anything is possible one stroke at a time", "Bijou", "Certified Zentangle Teacher", "CZT"®, "Zentangle Apprentice"®, and "Zentomology" are trademarks, service marks, or certification marks of Rick Roberts, Maria Thomas, and/or Zentangle Inc.

PERMISSION TO COPY ARTWORKS: The written instructions, designs, patterns, and projects in this book are intended for the personal use of the reader and may be reproduced for that purpose only. Any other use, especially commercial use, is forbidden under law without the written permission of the copyright holder.

All the tangles in this book are Zentangle originals created by Rick Roberts and Maria Thomas, apart from: Aztec (page 103) by Hannah Geddes CZT, Crezn't (page 43) and Gingham (page 46) by Margaret Bremner CZT, Daviso (page 125) by Katie Crommett CZT, Hollibaugh (page 63) by Molly Hollibaugh, Sand Swirl (page 75) by Karry Heun, and Vache 1 (page 27) and Wartz (page 18) by Genevieve Crabe CZT.

ARCTURUS

This edition published in 2016 by Arcturus Publishing Limited
26/27 Bickels Yard, 151–153 Bermondsey Street,
London SE1 3HA

Copyright © Arcturus Holdings Limited

ISBN: 978-1-78599-694-8
CH005151NT
Supplier 26, Date 0916, Print run 5267

Step-outs and Zentangle Inspired Artworks by Hannah Geddes
Text by Catherine Ard
Outline illustrations by Katy Jackson
Designed by Trudi Webb
Edited by Frances Evans

Printed in China

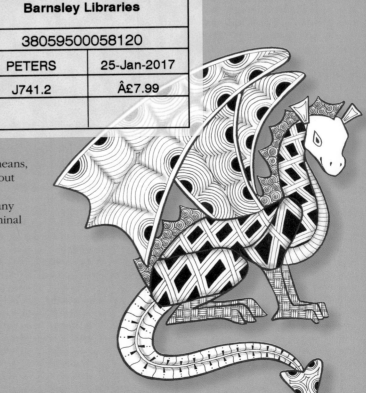

Contents

What is Zentangle?

Zentangle is a drawing method created by Rick Roberts and Maria Thomas. It teaches you how to create beautiful pieces of art using simple patterns called tangles. Tangling is a really fun, relaxing way to get creative, and it brings out the artist in everyone. You can tangle wherever and whenever the mood takes you!

This book will show you how to draw a wonderful collection of tangles and create your own Zentangle Inspired Artworks ("ZIAs"). Each chapter is based around a theme and features tangles that suit that theme particularly well, but you can mix and match tangles from across the book however you like. This introduction explains a few of the things that will be useful to help you get started.

Pens and Pencils

Pencils are good for drawing "strings" (page 6) and for adding shade to your tangles. A 01 (0.25-mm) black pen is good for fine lines. Use a 05 (0.45-mm) or 08 (0.50-mm) pen to fill in bigger areas. You can use paints to brighten up your art, too!

Paper

Tangles are usually drawn on a square 9-cm (3.5-inch) tile made of thin cardboard. You can use any kind of paper, but if you want to make your tangles really special use good quality art paper. Have some tracing paper on hand so you can trace images to use as outlines for your Zentangle Inspired Artworks.

Useful Words

There are some special words you might come across when you tangle. A "highlight" is a gap in the lines of your tangles. They can make your art look like it's sparkling! An "aura" is a line traced around the inside or outside of your tangle. Use auras to add a sense of movement to your pictures.

Strings, Tangles, and ZIAs

The Zentangle method begins with drawing "strings". These are pencil lines that separate spaces on your paper. The spaces are then filled with "tangles". All of the tangles have names. Throughout this book, you'll find step-by-step projects that show you how to create Zentangle Inspired Artworks ("ZIAs"). All of these start with a simple outline, with the strings already drawn in. Let's have a go with this pretty Chinese lantern picture.

1. Start with the outline of a Chinese lantern. I've drawn strings across the lantern to split the space up, and to add extra detail to the top and bottom.

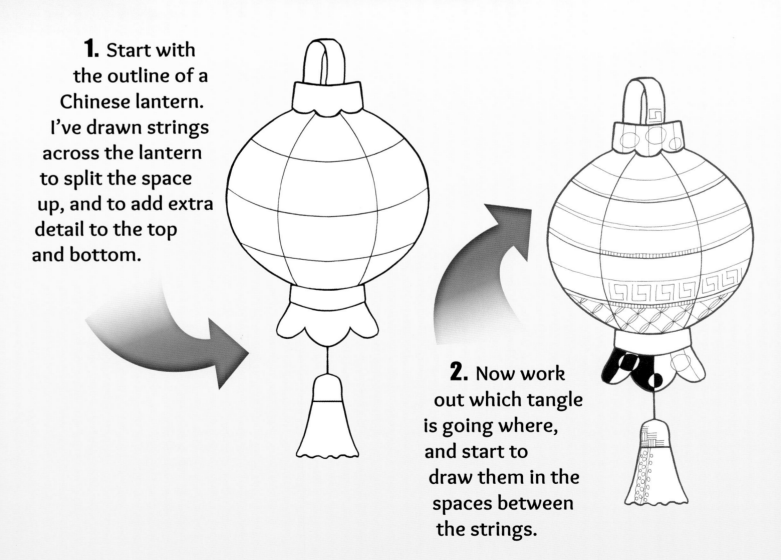

2. Now work out which tangle is going where, and start to draw them in the spaces between the strings.

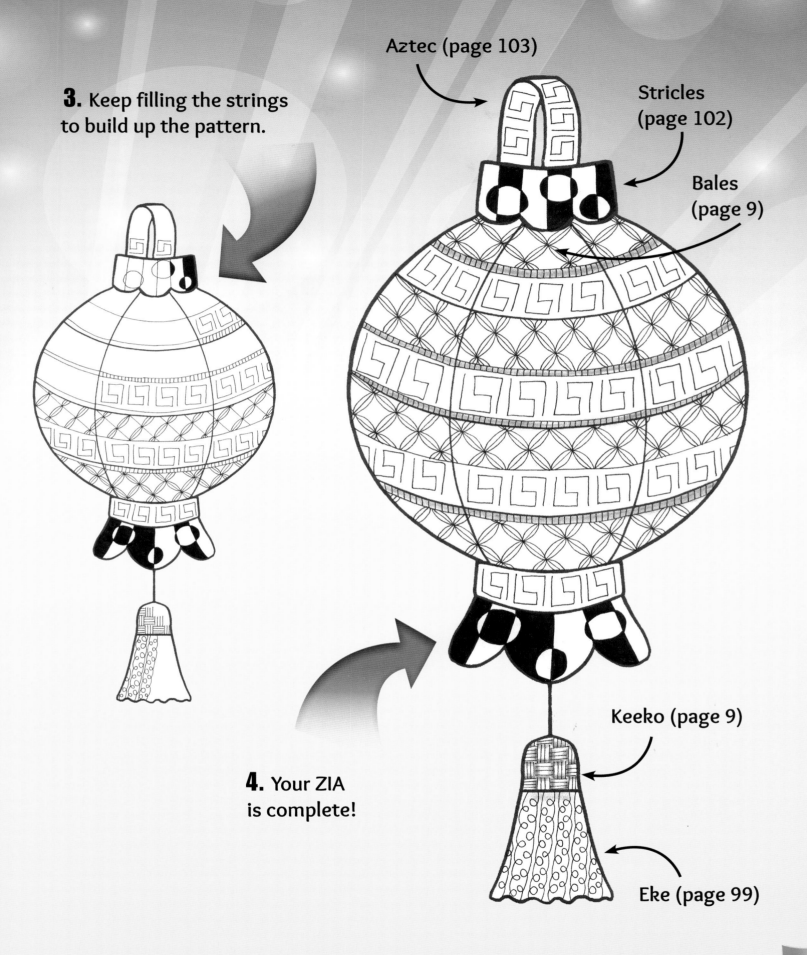

3. Keep filling the strings to build up the pattern.

Aztec (page 103)

Stricles (page 102)

Bales (page 9)

4. Your ZIA is complete!

Keeko (page 9)

Eke (page 99)

Essential Tangles

These tangles are great ones to start with.
They'll come in handy throughout the book.

Printemps

1. Draw a dot in the middle of your page. Then begin to draw a small spiral starting from the dot.

2. Continue drawing your spiral. You can make it as small or as big as you like.

3. Once the spiral is the size that you want, turn the line in to close up the shape. You should have a smooth circle around the edge.

4. Add more spiral shapes around the first one.

5. Carry on drawing Printemps spirals until you have filled the space.

Tipple

  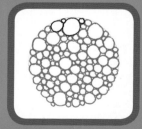 

1. Start by drawing a small circle on your paper.

2. Add a few more circles around the first one. They can be any size you like.

3. Keep drawing circles of different sizes until the chosen space is full.

4. Shade in the spaces between the circles to finish your tangle.

Bales

1. Draw evenly spaced diagonal lines across the paper.

2. Draw diagonal lines in the opposite direction to make a grid.

 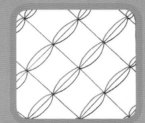

3. Draw bumps along the bottom of all of the lines you drew in step 1.

4. Then draw bumps along the top of these lines.

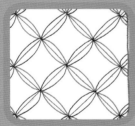 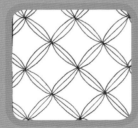

5. Repeat steps 3 and 4 on the diagonal lines that you drew in step 2.

6. Your pretty tangle is finished.

Keeko

 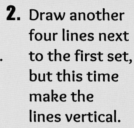

1. Draw four horizontal lines next to each other. They should be the same length and equally spaced apart.

2. Draw another four lines next to the first set, but this time make the lines vertical.

 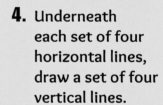

3. Repeat steps 1 and 2 until the row is complete.

4. Underneath each set of four horizontal lines, draw a set of four vertical lines.

5. Draw a set of four horizontal lines underneath each set of vertical lines.

6. Fill the chosen area, and then add some shading to finish it.

Cadent

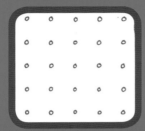 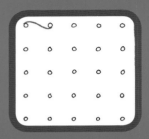  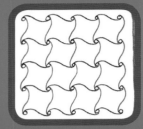 

1. Draw a grid made up of small circles.

2. Draw a curve from the top of the first circle to the bottom of the second circle.

3. Repeat this pattern across each horizontal row of circles.

4. Now, use the same pattern to join up the vertical lines of circles.

5. Your Cadent tangle is complete.

'Nzeppel

 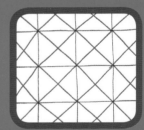 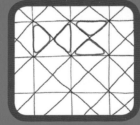  

1. Draw horizontal and vertical lines over the paper to make a grid.

2. Now draw diagonal lines in both directions over the paper. They should be evenly spaced so they run through the middle of each square in the grid.

3. Each square in the grid should now be split into four triangular sections. Draw around the shape of each triangle, but round off the corners to create this pebble-like effect.

4. Continue to fill each square with triangles, as shown.

5. Add some shading to finish your tangle.

Animals

Stealthy Jaguar

A jaguar's spotty markings keep it hidden as it slinks through the jungle. Follow these steps to create you own big cat with a cool Zentangle coat.

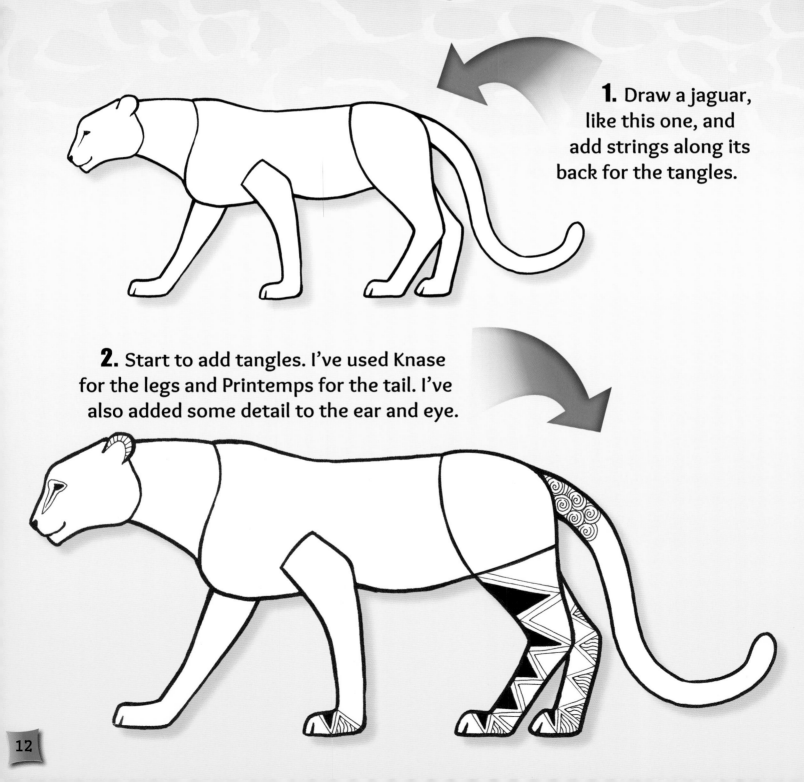

1. Draw a jaguar, like this one, and add strings along its back for the tangles.

2. Start to add tangles. I've used Knase for the legs and Printemps for the tail. I've also added some detail to the ear and eye.

3. Add tangles to the body, section by section. Diva Dance works well here as it shows off the muscular shape of the animal.

TANGLE KEY
Diva Dance: page 14
Knase: page 15
Printemps: page 8

4. Work carefully on the face, making sure the line of the mouth can still be seen.

Diva Dance

This wavy, spotty tangle works well for anything that is on the move.

1. Start by drawing a wavy line, then leave a gap and draw another one to match. Add a bump to the second line and fill it in.

2. Draw another pair of lines that flow around the bump. Keep the lines evenly spaced apart. Add another bump on a different part of the second line and fill it in.

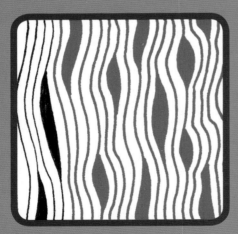

3. Continue this pattern, adding pairs of lines with a bump somewhere along the second line.

4. Make some bumps longer, some shorter, and some wider so that your tangle has a natural look.

Knase

This spiky tangle will give any picture the edge.

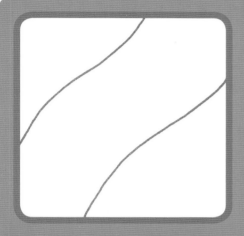

1. Start by drawing two evenly spaced diagonal lines.

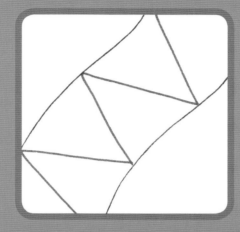

2. Draw a zigzag between the two lines.

3. Draw triangles inside the top row of the zigzag and fill them in. Now draw triangles inside the bottom row of the zigzag.

4. Finally, fill each triangle in the bottom row with wavy lines.

5. Your tangle is complete!

Tangle Tip!
The zigzags in Knase would be perfect for a tiger or zebra picture!

15

Snappy Crocodile

Crocodiles like to sunbathe on the banks of muddy rivers. Learn how to create this striking croc with tangles that show off its spiky tail and scaly skin.

1. Carefully copy this crocodile outline. Draw strings along its body for your tangles.

2. Start to fill the spaces between the strings. I've used Avreal on the tail and the top of the back to give a jagged texture.

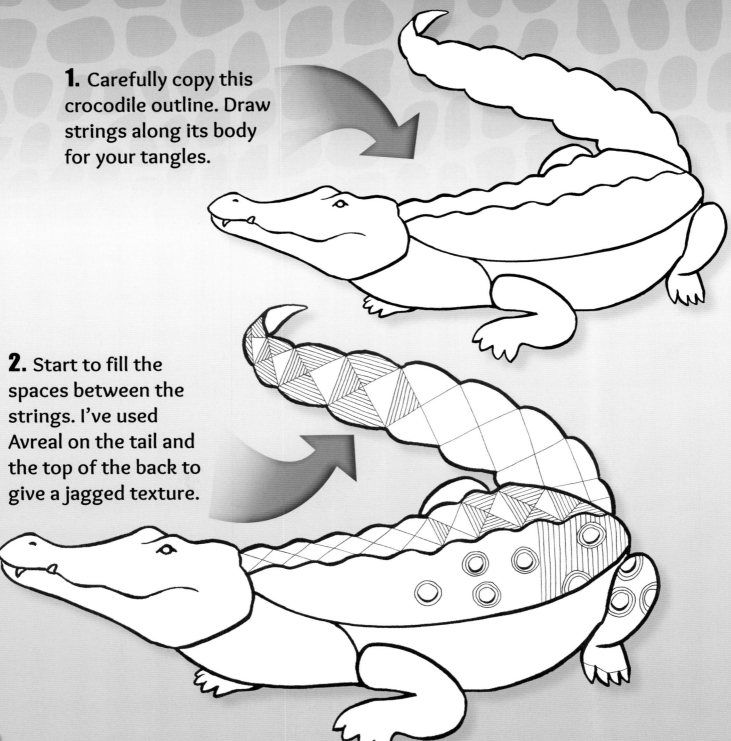

3. Choose a contrasting tangle for the rest of the crocodile. I've used Wartz on the body and legs to give a scaly look.

TANGLE KEY

Avreal: page 19
Wartz: page 18

4. Draw a line around the eye and below the mouth. Leave these areas untangled when you work on the crocodile's face. I left the claws blank, too.

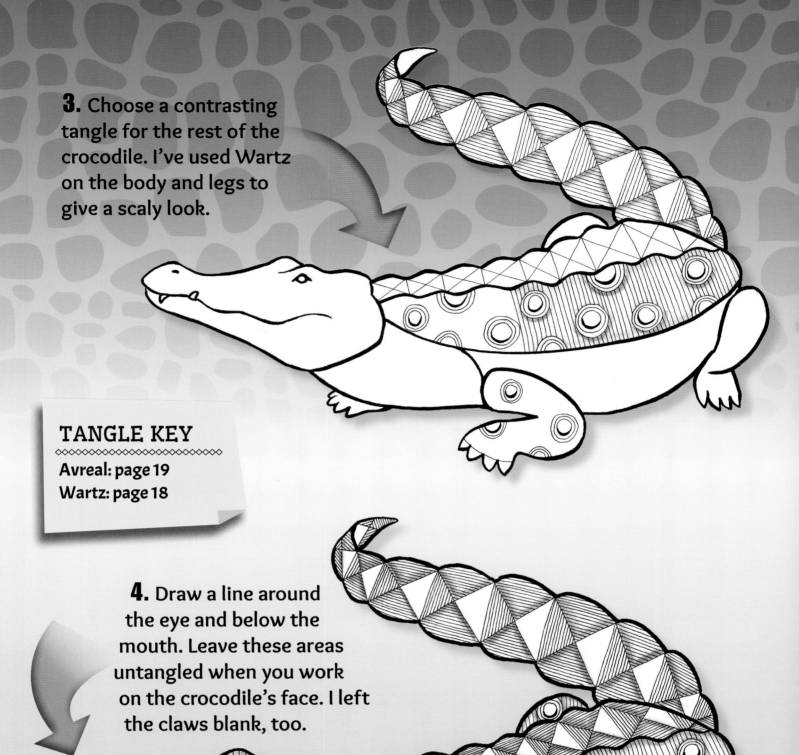

Wartz

Stripes contrast with the circles on this tangle to create a brilliant, bumpy texture.

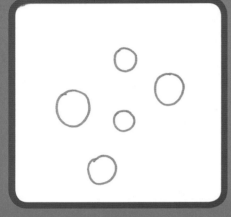

1. Draw a group of different-sized circles in the middle of the page.

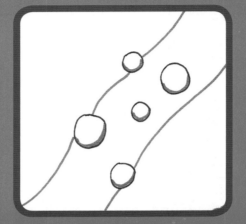

2. Make the pen line thicker at the bottom of each circle. Now add two wavy lines going across the middle of the page. When you reach a circle, stop the line and then continue it on the other side.

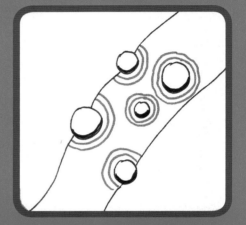

3. Draw two more circles, called "auras", around each circle. When a circle overlaps a line, only draw the aura around the part that is inside the line.

4. Draw stripes to fill the area inside the wavy lines. Stop the lines at the edge of each circle.

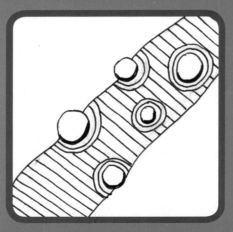

5. Your tangle is ready. You could add shade along the edges of the wavy lines and around the circles to make them stand out.

Tangle Tip!
This knobbly tangle would be ideal for a toad picture. You could use it to create a tree bark texture, too.

Avreal

The strong shapes and sharp edges in this tangle
are perfect for spikes and spines.

1. Start by drawing two pairs
of slightly curved lines with
a space in between, like this.

2. Draw a zigzag between the
pairs of lines.

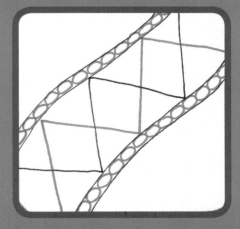

3. Draw another zigzag line
from the opposite side to
make a row of diamonds.
Fill the areas between the
pairs of lines with ovals.

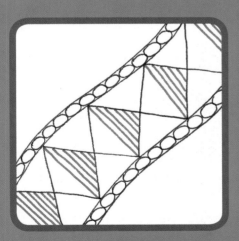

4. Fill the right half of
each diamond with
straight lines.

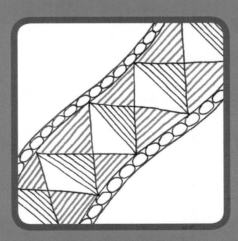

5. Then add horizontal lines above and
below the diamonds. When you
reach a diamond, stop the line and
then continue it on the other side.

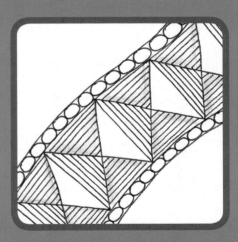

6. Add shading to finish
your tangle.

19

Playful Squirrel

Squirrels have big, bushy tails to help them balance as they leap through the trees. Follow these steps to create your own cute squirrel with a beautiful tail.

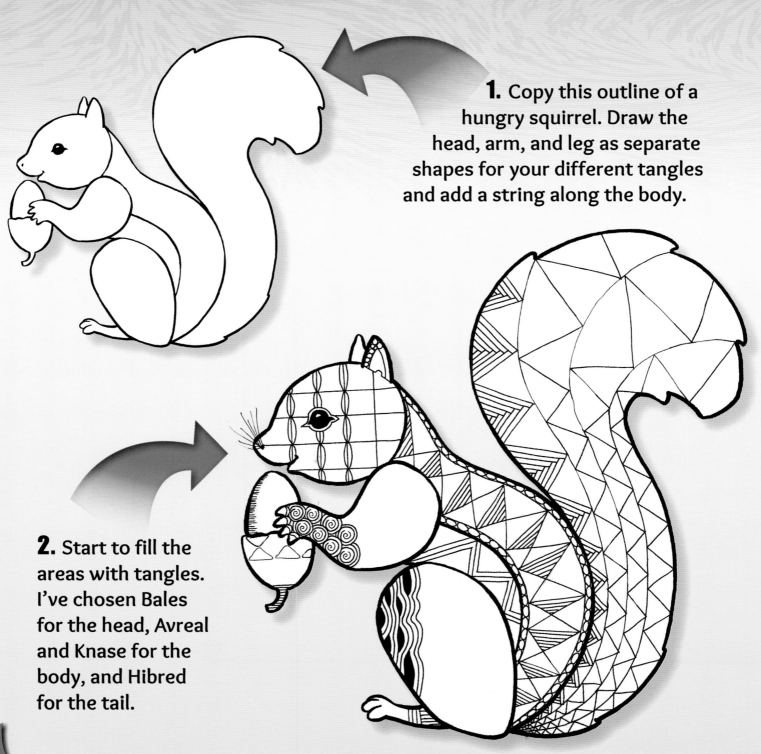

1. Copy this outline of a hungry squirrel. Draw the head, arm, and leg as separate shapes for your different tangles and add a string along the body.

2. Start to fill the areas with tangles. I've chosen Bales for the head, Avreal and Knase for the body, and Hibred for the tail.

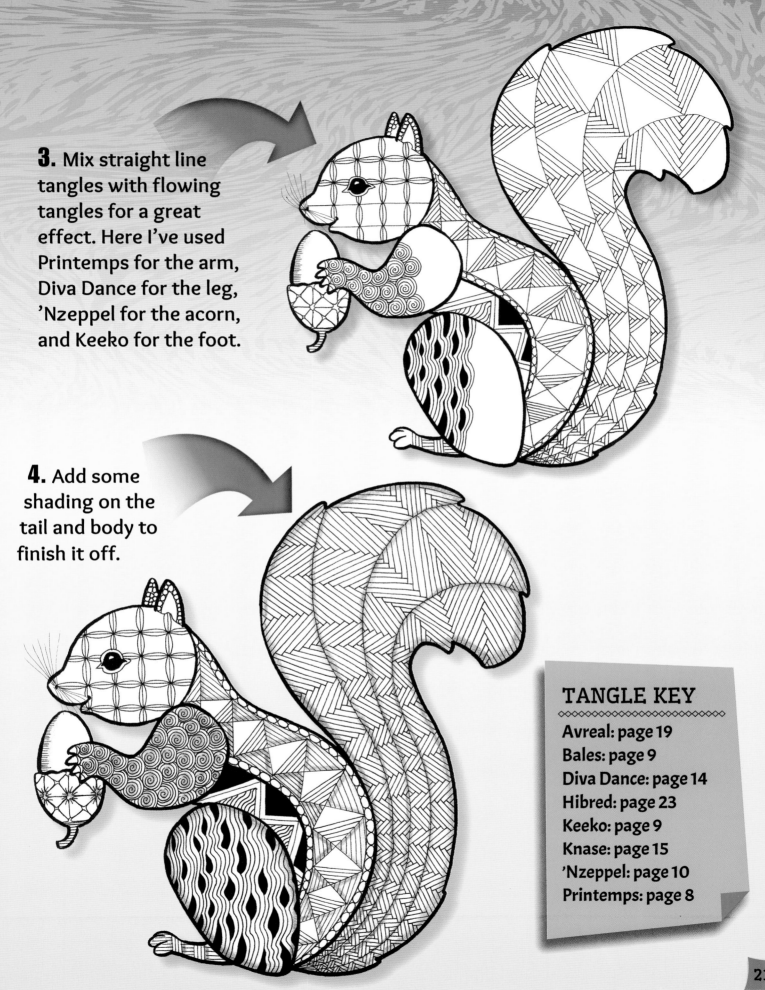

3. Mix straight line tangles with flowing tangles for a great effect. Here I've used Printemps for the arm, Diva Dance for the leg, 'Nzeppel for the acorn, and Keeko for the foot.

4. Add some shading on the tail and body to finish it off.

TANGLE KEY

Avreal: page 19
Bales: page 9
Diva Dance: page 14
Hibred: page 23
Keeko: page 9
Knase: page 15
'Nzeppel: page 10
Printemps: page 8

Ennies

Try this pretty tangle of pebbles framed with petals for a natural touch.

1. Draw a petal shape lying on its side at the bottom of the space.

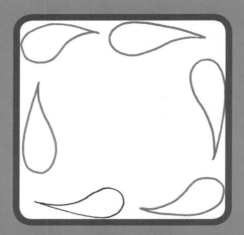

2. Add more petal shapes around the outside.

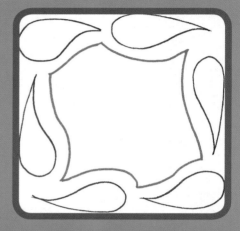

3. Draw an inner frame, following the outlines of the petals.

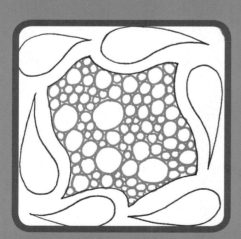

4. Add lots of closely-packed circles inside the frame, making them all different sizes.

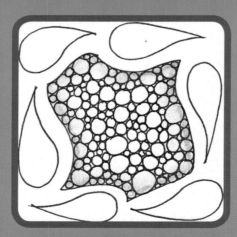

5. Shade along the inside edges of the frame with a pencil and smudge with your finger to finish.

Tangle Tip!

The tightly packed circles and loose petal frame create a nice contrast. Use this tangle on parts of your picture that you want to stand out!

Hibred

Weave some magic into your artwork with this tidy, criss-cross tangle.

1. Draw two pairs of lines with a space in between, like this.

2. Draw a zigzag between the pairs of lines.

3. Add a line inside each "V" of the zigzag, starting on the left.

4. Now, add a line inside each "V" on the right.

5. Continue to add lines, first on the left, then on the right, to fill the space.

6. Now start to add lines below the "Vs", starting on the right.

7. Now add a line on the left. Continue adding lines on the right and then the left until the space is filled.

8. Shade along the edges with a pencil and smudge it with your finger.

Stately Stag

Male deer grow a pair of majestic antlers every spring. Follow these simple steps to create your very own Zentangle-inspired stag, with a beautiful set of antlers!

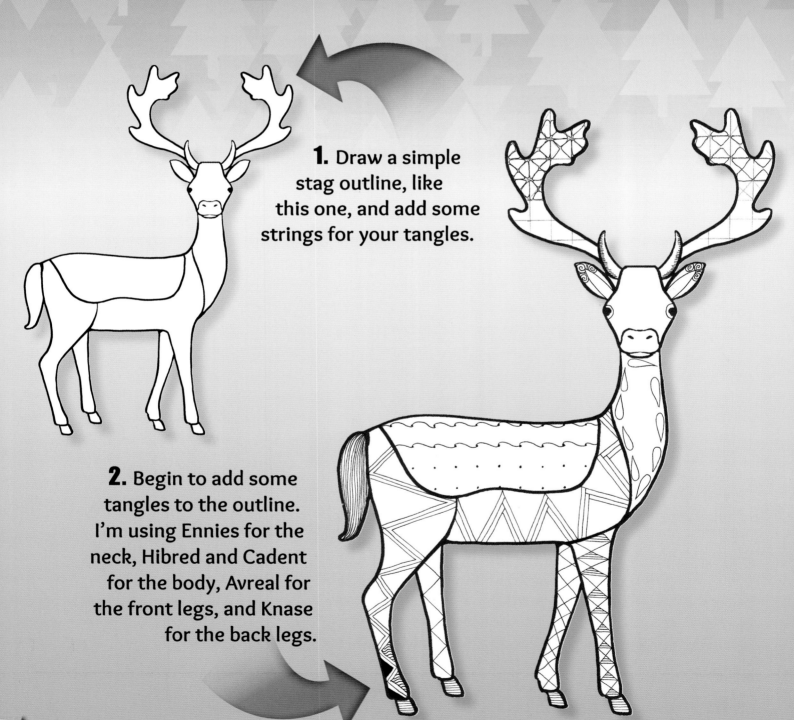

1. Draw a simple stag outline, like this one, and add some strings for your tangles.

2. Begin to add some tangles to the outline. I'm using Ennies for the neck, Hibred and Cadent for the body, Avreal for the front legs, and Knase for the back legs.

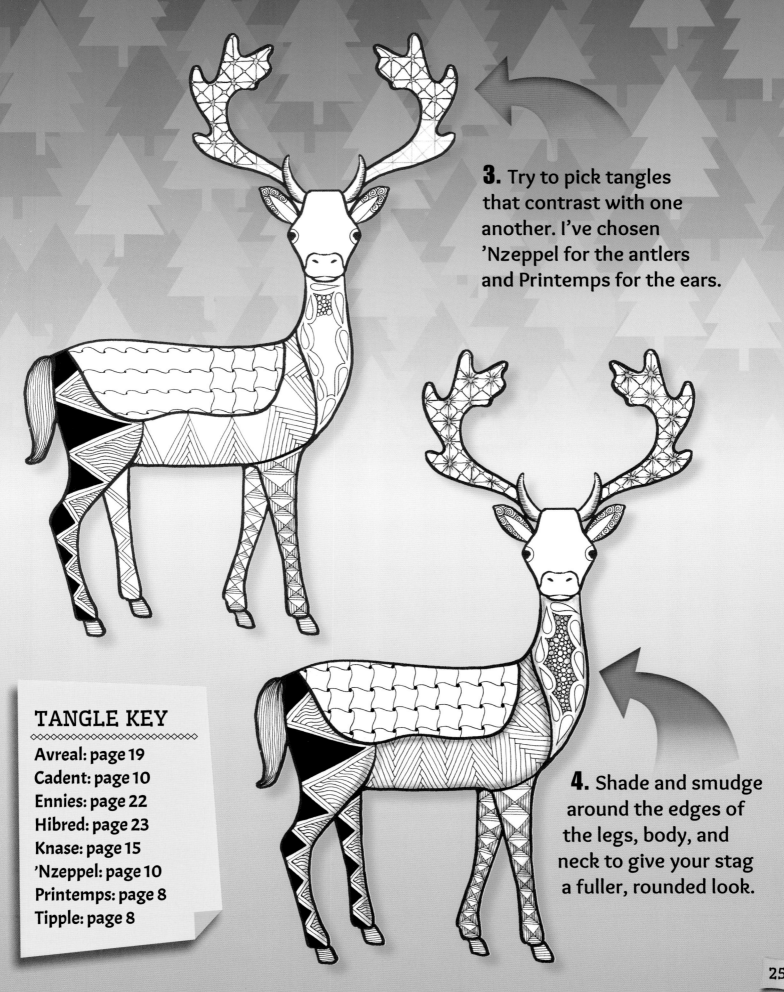

3. Try to pick tangles that contrast with one another. I've chosen 'Nzeppel for the antlers and Printemps for the ears.

4. Shade and smudge around the edges of the legs, body, and neck to give your stag a fuller, rounded look.

TANGLE KEY

Cubine

Check out the squares on this tangle! It's perfect for giving large areas a bold look.

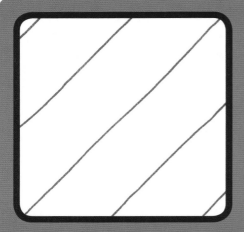

1. Draw evenly spaced diagonal lines from left to right across the paper.

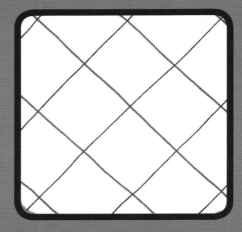

2. Now add diagonal lines going in the opposite direction.

3. Draw a small box in the right-hand corner of each square and fill it in.

4. Add a line from the left-hand corner of each square to the right-hand corner of each box.

5. Shade above the line in each square to finish your tangle.

Tangle Tip!
Try changing the size of the grid to create a different look. You could experiment with vertical or curved lines, too!

Vache 1

This patterned tangle creates a texture that is perfect for giraffe's fur or tough rhino skin.

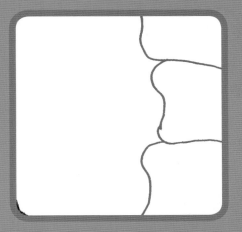

1. Start by drawing loose shapes on your paper. They can be any size or shape you like, but the edges must touch.

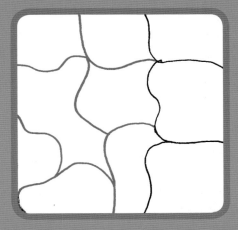

2. Draw more shapes until you have filled up the whole area.

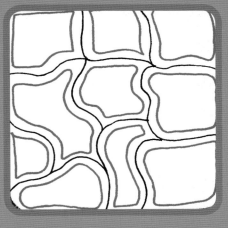

3. Inside each shape, draw a smaller shape that follows the same outline.

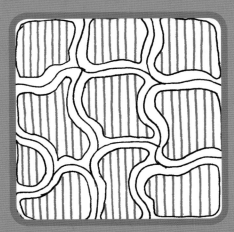

4. Fill each smaller shape with vertical lines that are evenly spaced apart.

5. Your tangle is complete!

Gentle Rhino

Rhinos like to keep cool by wallowing in muddy waterholes. Give your rhino a Zentangle makeover and swap the mud for some amazing tangles!

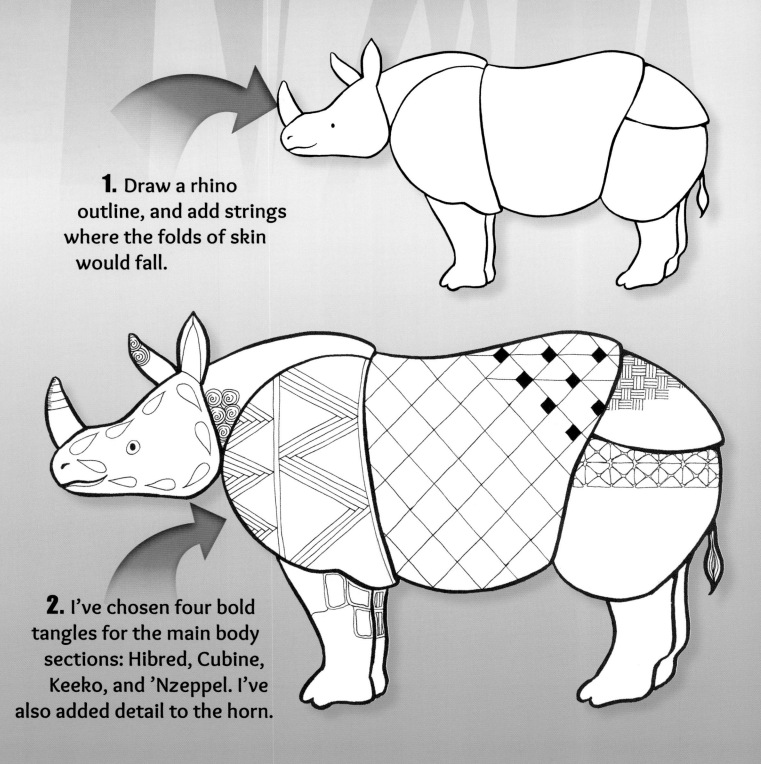

1. Draw a rhino outline, and add strings where the folds of skin would fall.

2. I've chosen four bold tangles for the main body sections: Hibred, Cubine, Keeko, and 'Nzeppel. I've also added detail to the horn.

TANGLE KEY

Cubine: page 26
Ennies: page 22
Hibred: page 23
Printemps: page 8
'Nzeppel: page 10
Keeko: page 9
Vache 1: page 27

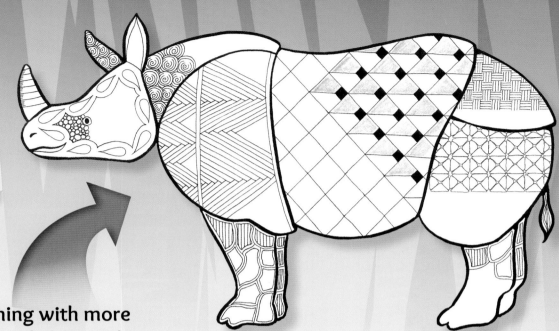

3. Pick something with more detail for the head. I've used Ennies for the face and Printemps for the ears and shoulder.

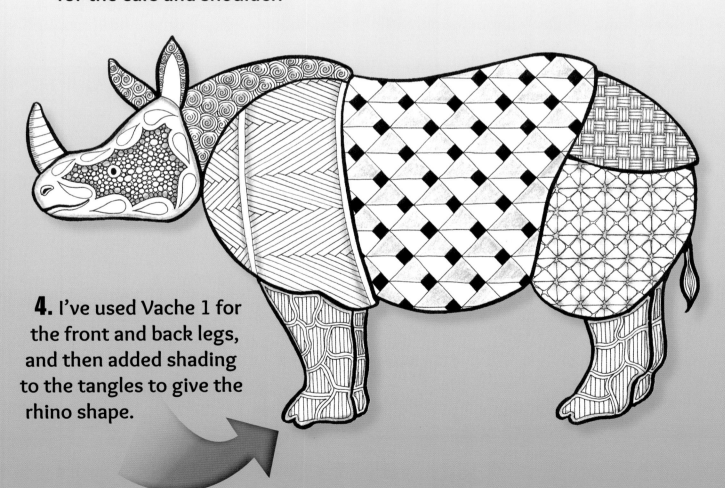

4. I've used Vache 1 for the front and back legs, and then added shading to the tangles to give the rhino shape.

Tangle Time!

Use some really wild tangles to complete these animals!

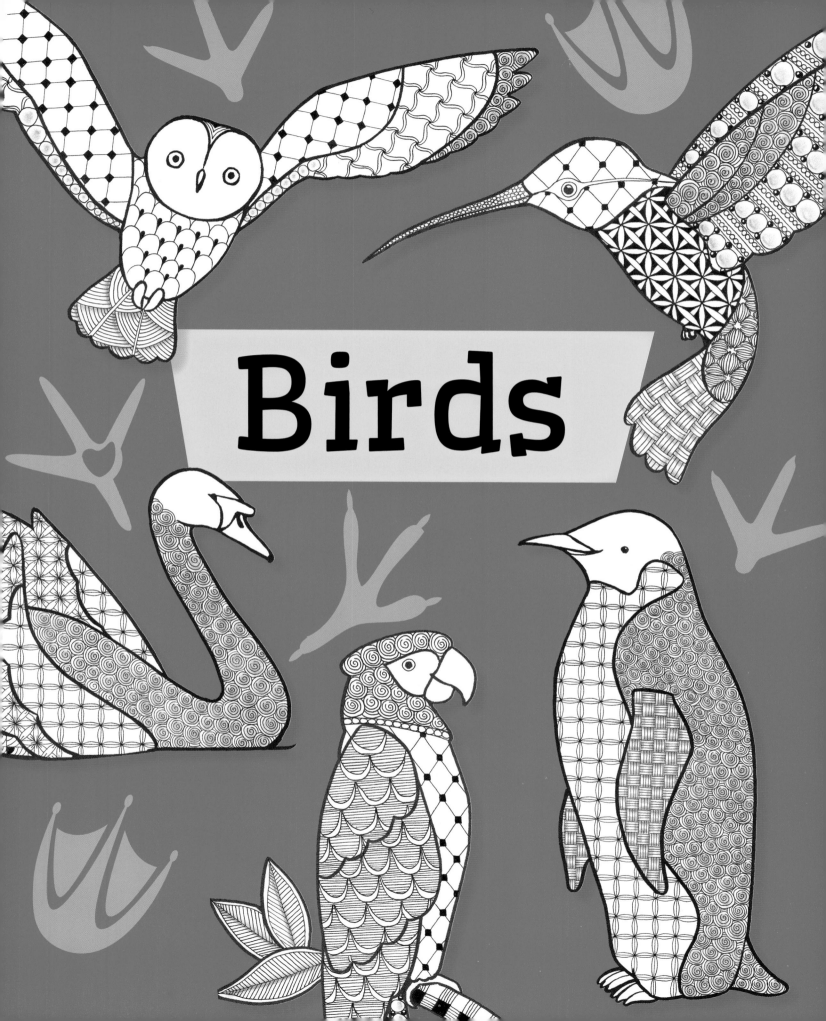

Birds

Perfect Penguin

With their white shirts and black jackets, penguins look like they are dressed for dinner! Follow these steps to give a plain penguin a stylish new look.

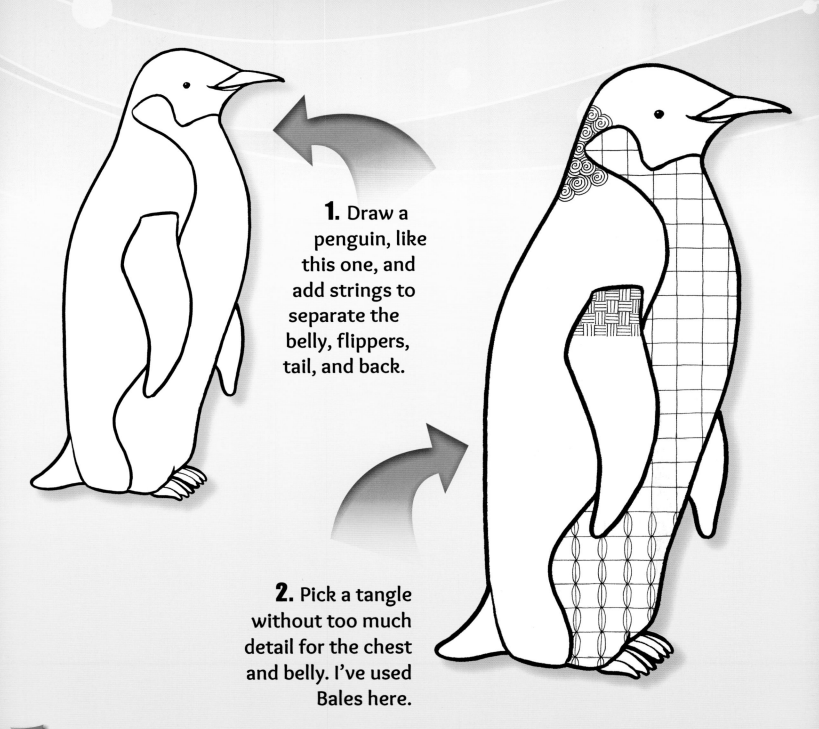

1. Draw a penguin, like this one, and add strings to separate the belly, flippers, tail, and back.

2. Pick a tangle without too much detail for the chest and belly. I've used Bales here.

3. Use more detailed tangles for the darker areas. I've chosen Keeko for the flippers and Printemps for the tail and back.

TANGLE KEY
Bales: page 9
Keeko: page 9
Printemps: page 8

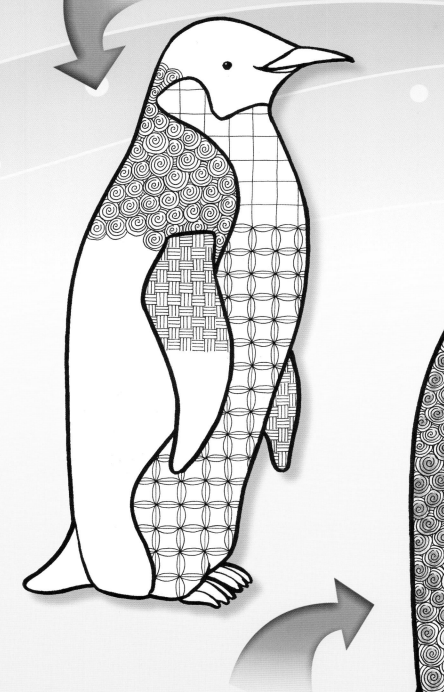

4. Add some shading to the back and flippers to finish your penguin picture.

Fife

This woven mass of pretty petals brings a floral touch to any picture.

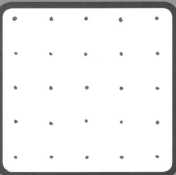

1. Start by drawing a grid of dots, like this.

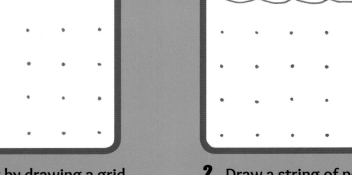

2. Draw a string of petals across the top row, using the dots as a guide.

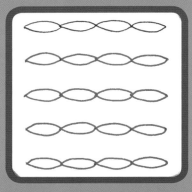

3. Repeat with a string of petals on each row.

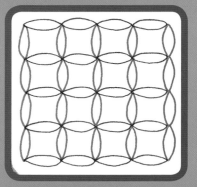

4. Now add vertical strings of petals to make a grid of overlapping circles.

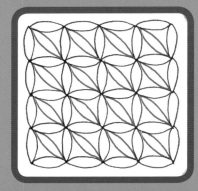

5. Inside each circle there is a bendy square. Add a petal inside each one, stretching from the top left to the bottom right.

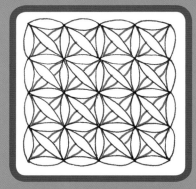

6. Now draw petals going in the opposite direction inside each square. When you meet a petal, stop the line and continue it on the other side.

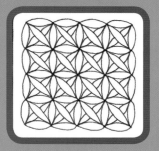

7. Your tangle is ready. You could add lines to the middle of each flower for extra twinkle.

Beelight

Make your animal pictures really stand out with this eye-catching tangle.

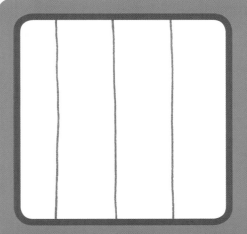

1. Draw evenly spaced vertical lines over the page.

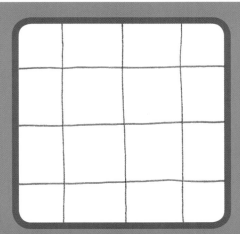

2. Add the same number of horizontal lines to make a grid of squares.

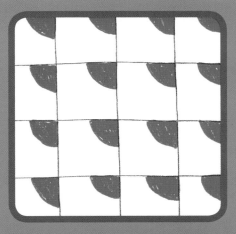

3. Draw a quarter of a circle in the top right-hand corner of each square and then fill it in with pen.

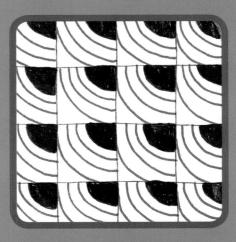

4. Add curved lines around each quarter circle to fill every square.

5. Your Beelight tangle is complete.

Tangle Tip!
Leave a small gap (called a "highlight") between a few of the curved lines to give Beelight some texture. Look at the swan's feathers on page 37.

Elegant Swan

Swans glide effortlessly through the water with their elegant necks held high. You can create your own graceful Zentangle swan in four simple steps.

1. Start by drawing the swan outline. Divide the wings into sections with curvy strings.

2. Begin to fill the wing sections with tangles. I've used Bales, Fife, and Beelight.

3. Continue tangling to complete the swan. I've chosen Printemps to represent the fluffy feathers on the neck and 'Nzeppel for the tail.

TANGLE KEY

Bales: page 9
Beelight: page 35
Fife: page 34
Printemps: page 8
'Nzeppel: page 10

4. Shade with a pencil on the neck and tail, and smudge with your finger to finish.

Tagh

This tangle creates a lovely feathery effect, so it's perfect for a bird ZIA!

1. Start by drawing a petal shape in the bottom left-hand corner of the paper.

2. Add another petal on either side of the first one.

3. Draw a row of narrow bumps above the petals. Begin and end each line in the middle of the shape in the row below.

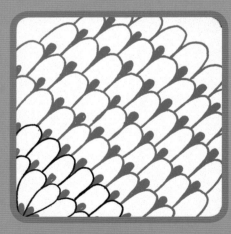

4. Carry on drawing more rows of bumps to fill the area. Then draw a small petal in the gap at the bottom of each shape and fill them in with your pen.

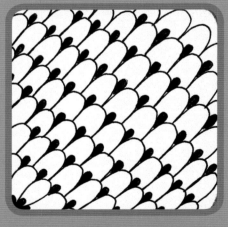

5. Your Tagh tangle is finished!

Tangle Tip!
You could use this tangle on all sorts of bird pictures. It would also make great scales for fish!

38

Shattuck

The overlapping layers in Shattuck create a striking effect on wings and tail feathers.

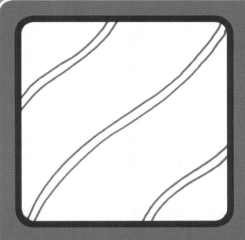

1. Draw three pairs of wavy lines, as shown, to make bands. Space the bands evenly across the paper.

2. Draw a slightly curved diagonal line between a pair of bands, and then add several more lines above it.

3. Draw several lines going in the opposite direction below the first set of lines. Add a set of lines between the next pair of bands.

4. Continue adding more sets of lines, changing direction each time until the area is full.

5. Add some pencil shading along the edges of each section to finish the tangle.

Magical Owl

Owls swoop silently through the darkness, gliding on their wide, outstretched wings. Draw your own awesome owl with a fine set of tangled feathers.

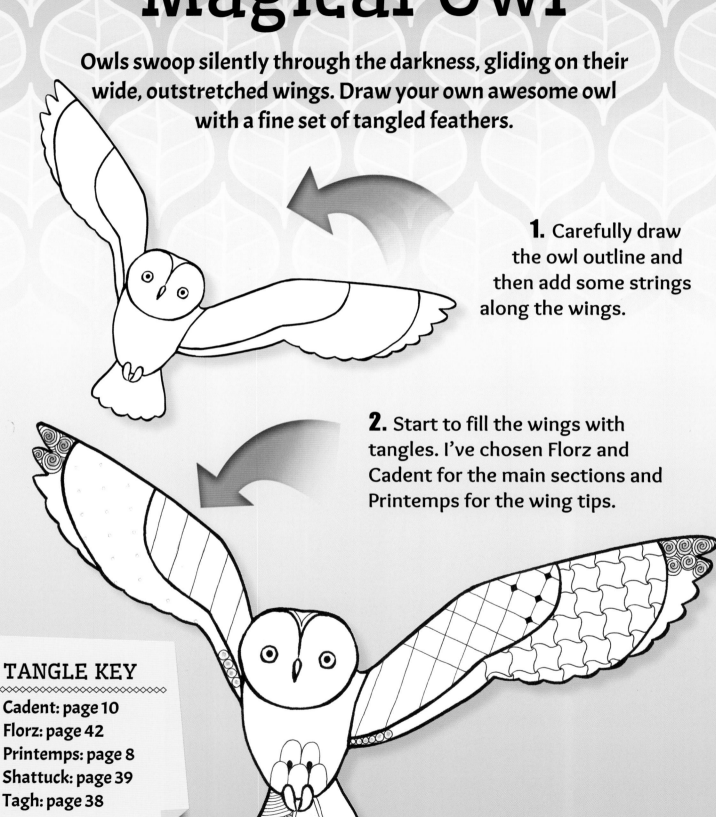

1. Carefully draw the owl outline and then add some strings along the wings.

2. Start to fill the wings with tangles. I've chosen Florz and Cadent for the main sections and Printemps for the wing tips.

TANGLE KEY

Cadent: page 10
Florz: page 42
Printemps: page 8
Shattuck: page 39
Tagh: page 38

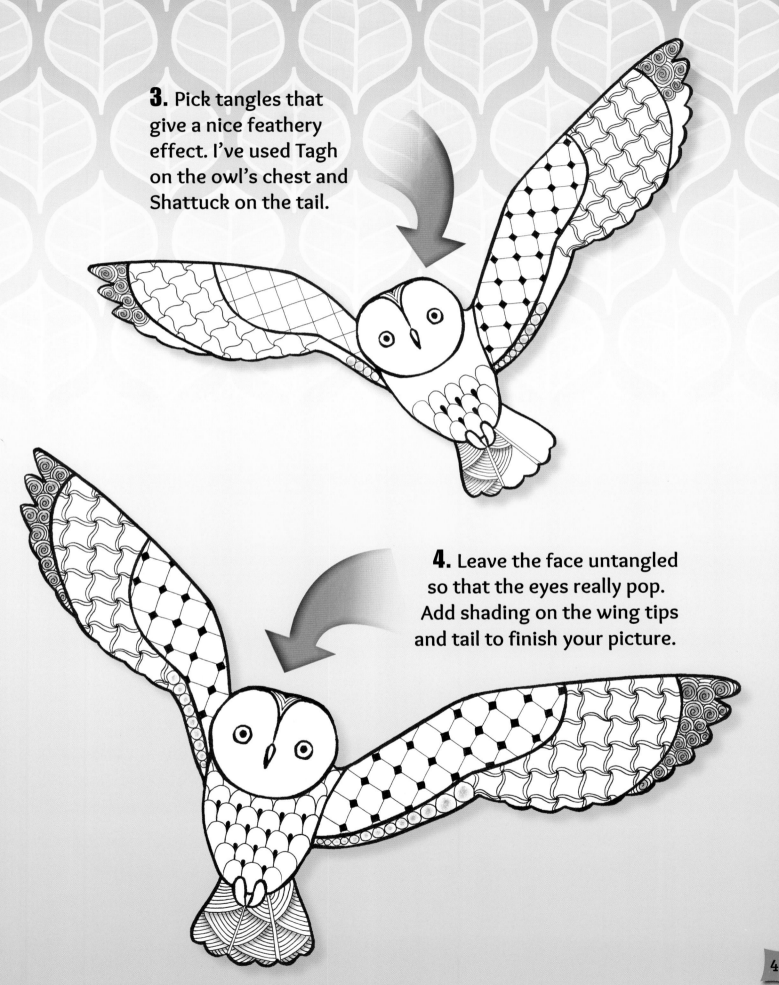

3. Pick tangles that give a nice feathery effect. I've used Tagh on the owl's chest and Shattuck on the tail.

4. Leave the face untangled so that the eyes really pop. Add shading on the wing tips and tail to finish your picture.

Florz

Combine this simple tangle with more elaborate ones for a really striking effect.

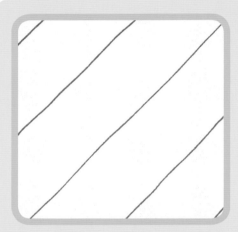

1. Start by drawing evenly spaced diagonal lines across the paper.

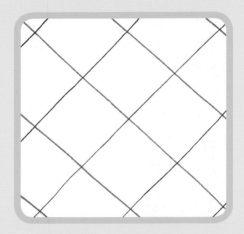

2. Now draw lines going in the opposite direction.

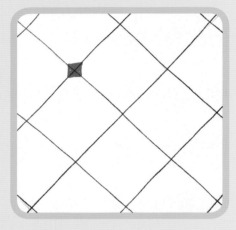

3. Draw a small square on a point where two lines cross. Fill in the square with pen.

4. Continue adding squares and filling them in.

5. Your tangle is finished!

Tangle Tip!

There are lots of ways you could vary this tangle. Try drawing a different shape where the lines cross, or using vertical instead of diagonal lines for the grid.

Crezn't

This lovely looping tangle works equally well for a fish's scales or a bird's feathers.

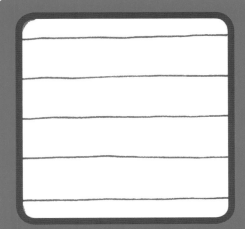

1. Draw horizontal lines across the paper.

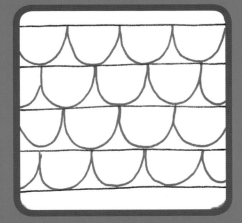

2. Draw a string of "U" shapes between the top two lines. Draw more "U" shapes in the rows below. Begin and end each "U" in the middle of a "U" in the row above.

3. Add a smaller "U" inside each big "U", making sure the lines meet at the top.

4. Draw evenly spaced horizontal lines in the spaces above and below the "U" shapes to create rows of little crescents.

5. Your tangle is ready!

Delicate Hummingbird

Tiny hummingbirds flash their bright feathers as they hover, collecting sweet nectar from flowers. Follow these steps to create a hummingbird covered in tangles from its beak to its tail.

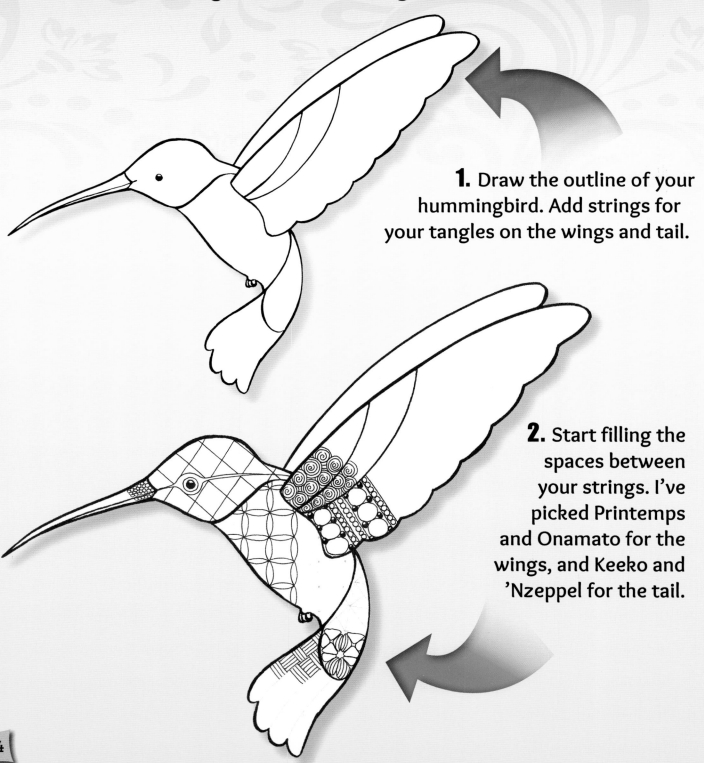

1. Draw the outline of your hummingbird. Add strings for your tangles on the wings and tail.

2. Start filling the spaces between your strings. I've picked Printemps and Onamato for the wings, and Keeko and 'Nzeppel for the tail.

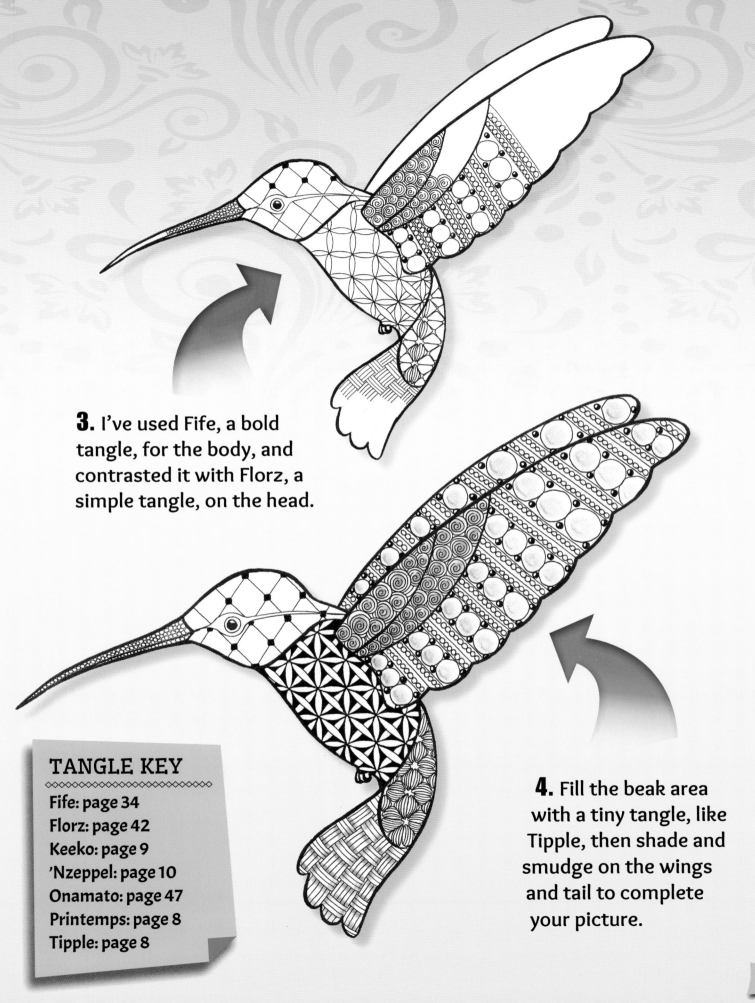

3. I've used Fife, a bold tangle, for the body, and contrasted it with Florz, a simple tangle, on the head.

TANGLE KEY

Fife: page 34
Florz: page 42
Keeko: page 9
'Nzeppel: page 10
Onamato: page 47
Printemps: page 8
Tipple: page 8

4. Fill the beak area with a tiny tangle, like Tipple, then shade and smudge on the wings and tail to complete your picture.

Gingham

This tangle ticks all the boxes when it comes to making a bold statement.

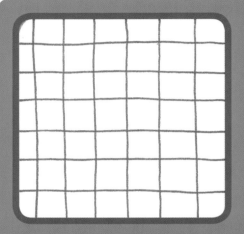

1. Start by drawing an odd number of evenly spaced vertical and horizontal lines across the paper to make a grid.

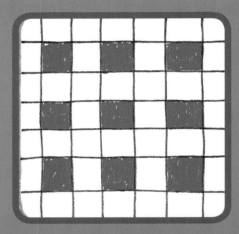

2. Now use your pen to fill in every other square in every other row.

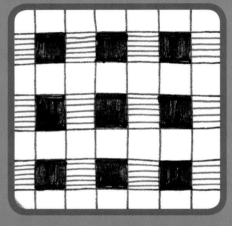

3. Along the rows with filled in squares, draw tightly-packed horizontal lines in the blank squares.

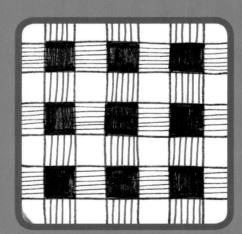

4. On the vertical rows with filled-in squares, draw tightly packed vertical lines in the blank squares.

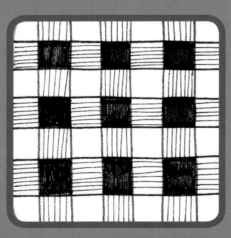

5. Your pretty checked pattern is complete!

Onamato

The pearly strings in this tangle add sparkle and shine to make every picture feel precious.

1. Start by drawing two pairs of lines to make bands. Make sure you leave a wide gap between them.

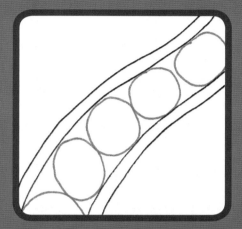

2. Draw tightly packed circles in between the bands. The circles should meet the lines at the top and bottom.

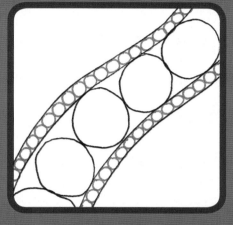

3. Fill the area inside each band with small, tightly packed circles.

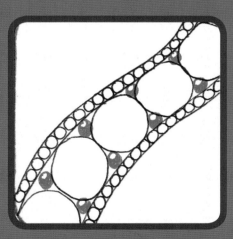

4. Draw small circles in the gaps between the big circles and fill them in, leaving a small highlight.

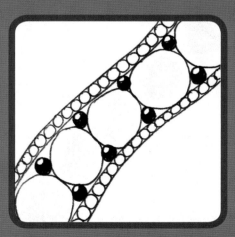

5. Your tangle is finished. You could add shade to the big circles, so they look like they are catching the light.

Tangle Tip!
This beautiful, simple tangle is a great way to add detail to tail feathers and wings.

Pretty Parrot

Parrots' bright feathers and loud squawks make them easy to find in the leafy jungles where they live. Pick the perfect tangles for your parrot and it will really attract attention!

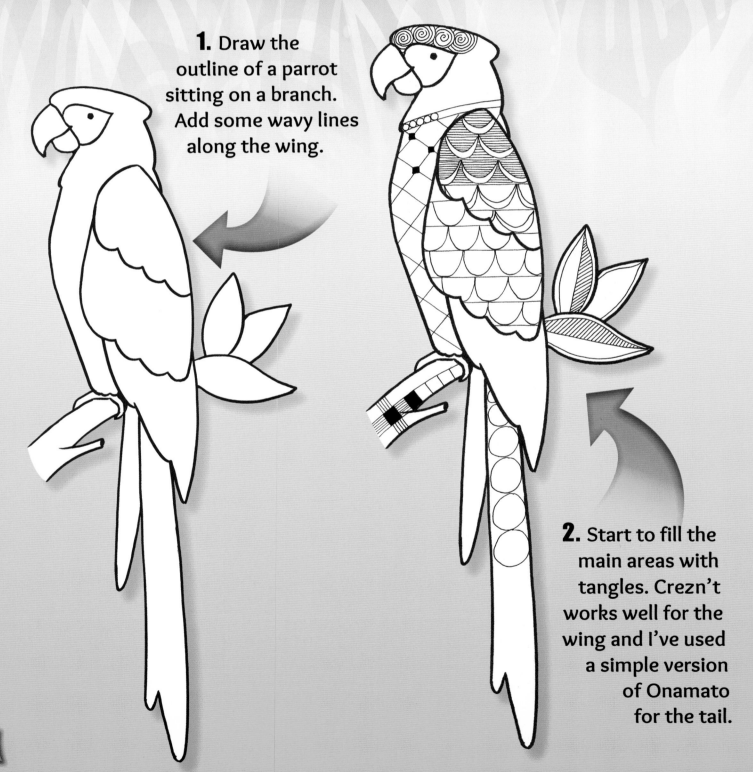

1. Draw the outline of a parrot sitting on a branch. Add some wavy lines along the wing.

2. Start to fill the main areas with tangles. Crezn't works well for the wing and I've used a simple version of Onamato for the tail.

3. Contrast the detailed tangles on the wing with something simple, like Florz, on the parrot's chest.

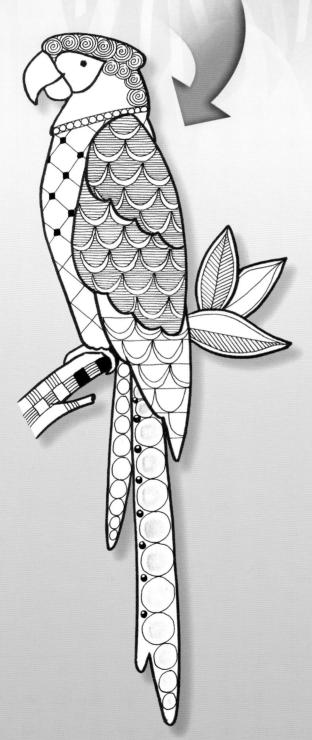

4. I've filled the branch with Gingham and the head with Printemps, finishing it off along the neck with a string of ovals. I added some detail on the leaves, too.

TANGLE KEY

Crezn't: page 43
Florz: page 42
Gingham: page 46
Onamato: page 47
Printemps: page 8

49

Tangle Time!

Fill these beautiful birds with your best tangles.

Insects
& Bugs

Spooky Spider

A spider waits patiently for an unsuspecting fly to get tangled in its web. Get stuck into some tangles of your own with this cool, creepy-crawly picture.

1. Draw a spider sitting on a web. The web has eight straight strands coming from the middle, with three layers of strings between the strands.

2. Rub out the edges of the strings and then start to add Fracas to the web.

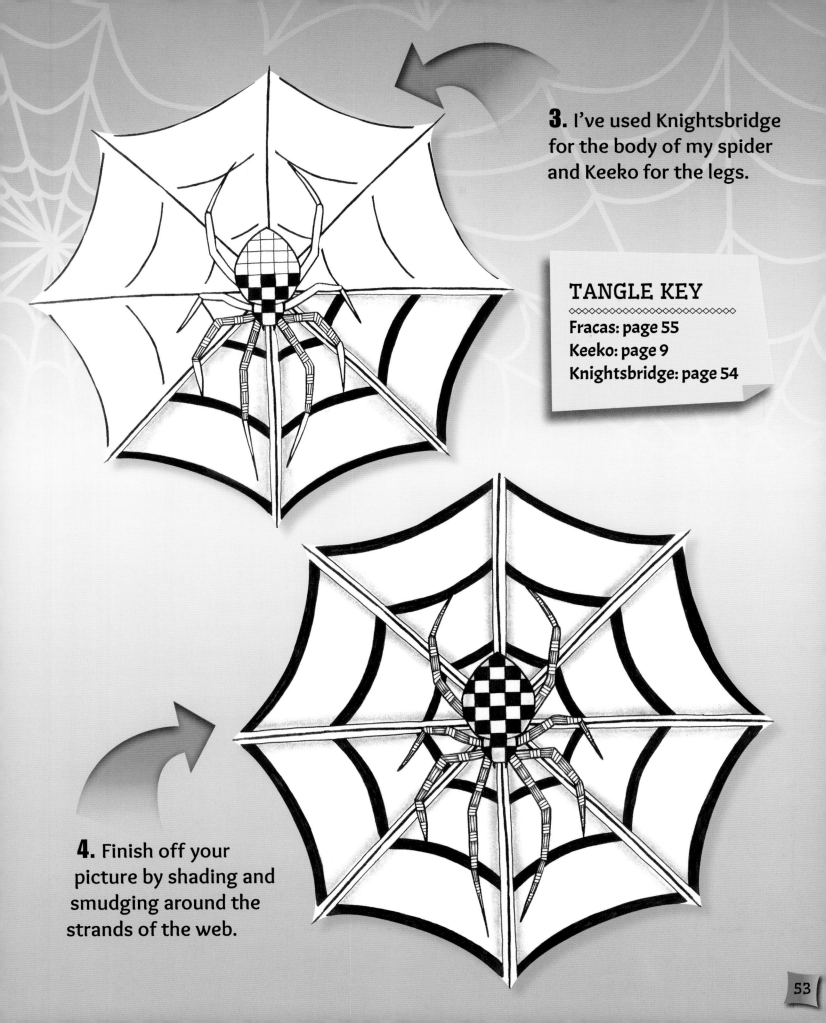

3. I've used Knightsbridge for the body of my spider and Keeko for the legs.

TANGLE KEY

Fracas: page 55
Keeko: page 9
Knightsbridge: page 54

4. Finish off your picture by shading and smudging around the strands of the web.

Knightsbridge

This tangle is super-easy and eye-catching, too!
Use it to add pizazz to any picture.

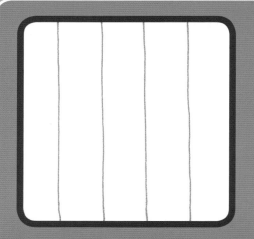

1. Start by drawing evenly spaced vertical lines across your paper.

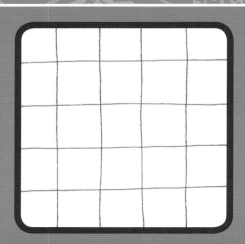

2. Now add the same number of horizontal lines to make a grid.

3. Use a pen to shade in every other square to create a check pattern.

4. Once you've mastered this simple grid pattern, you can customize it however you like.

Tangle Tip!
Change the look of this tangle by using diagonal lines to create your grid.

Fracas

Take a tip from our eight-legged friends and work this wonderful web tangle into your insect pictures.

1. Draw two diagonal lines from corner to corner to make an "X" on the paper.

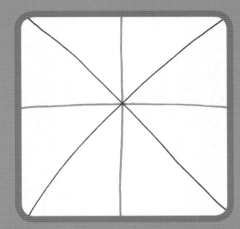

2. Add a vertical and a horizontal line across the middle.

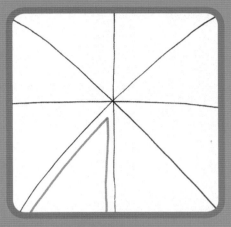

3. Draw lines inside one of the triangle sections as shown, leaving a small gap.

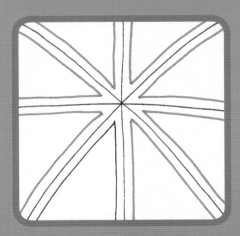

4. Repeat inside each triangle.

5. Now draw thick, evenly spaced stripes inside each triangle and fill them in.

6. Add some pencil shading along the edges of the triangles and blend to finish.

Stag Beetle

The male stag beetle has impressive jaws that look like a deer's antlers. Create your own beetle with tangled jaws and open wings, ready to fight or take flight!

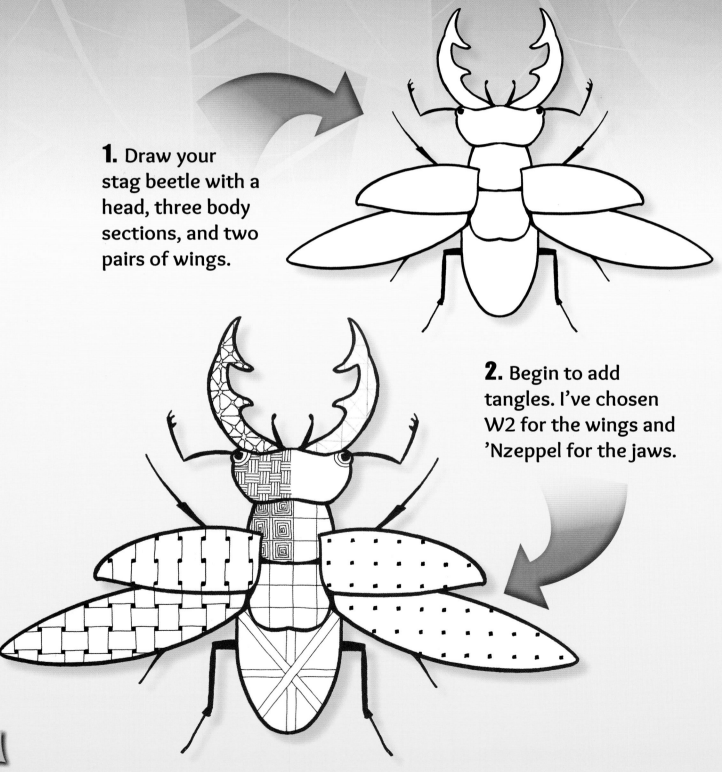

1. Draw your stag beetle with a head, three body sections, and two pairs of wings.

2. Begin to add tangles. I've chosen W2 for the wings and 'Nzeppel for the jaws.

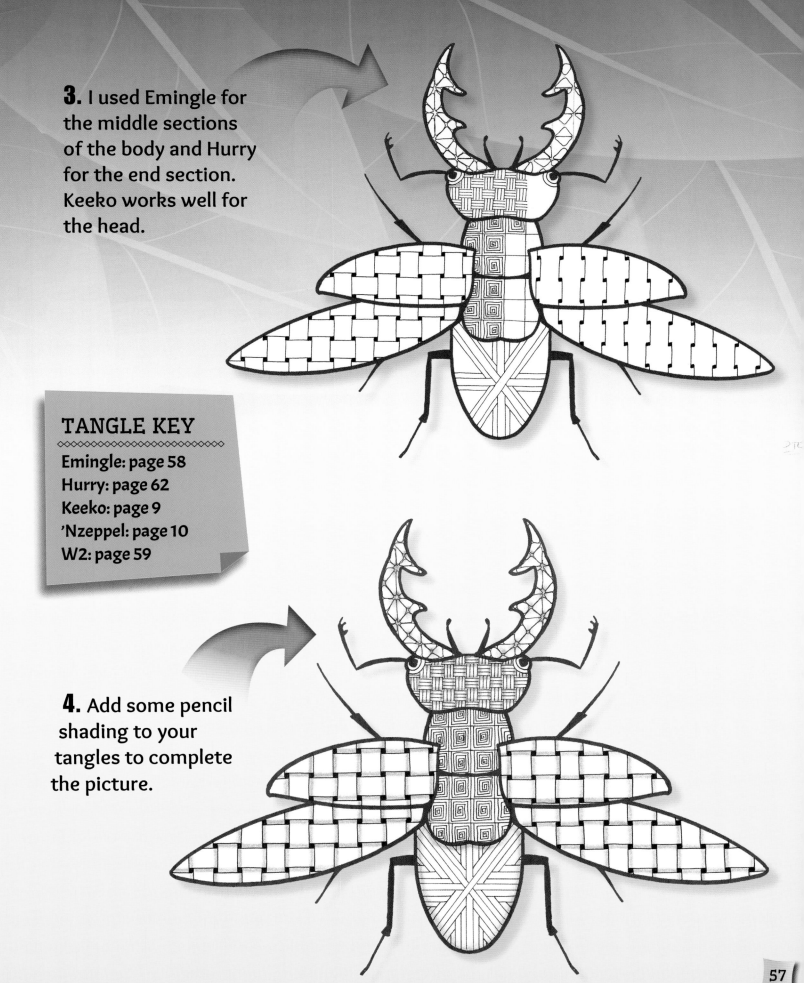

3. I used Emingle for the middle sections of the body and Hurry for the end section. Keeko works well for the head.

TANGLE KEY

Emingle: page 58
Hurry: page 62
Keeko: page 9
'Nzeppel: page 10
W2: page 59

4. Add some pencil shading to your tangles to complete the picture.

Emingle

Give your pictures a classic twist with this Greek-inspired spiral tangle.

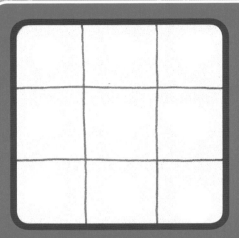

1. Draw evenly spaced vertical and horizontal lines to create a grid.

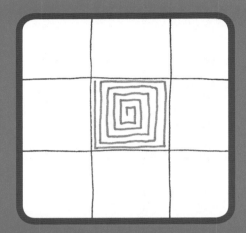

2. Starting in the middle of one of the squares, draw a straight-edged spiral to fill the shape.

3. Repeat in each square, drawing the spirals in the same direction each time.

4. Your tangle is complete!

Tangle Tip!
If you shade the middle of each spiral you can give Emingle a 3D effect!

W2

Carry off a really wacky look with this wonderful basket weave tangle!

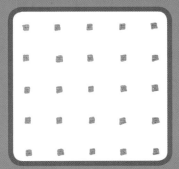

1. Start by drawing rows of small, evenly spaced squares. Fill in the squares with your pen.

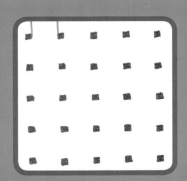

2. Starting in the top left, draw a line from the top of the paper to the right-hand edge of the first square. Now draw a line to the left-hand edge of the second square. Stop the lines at the bottom of the squares.

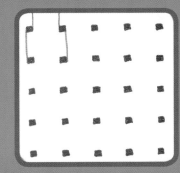

3. Add two more lines from the opposite edges of the squares, to the squares below.

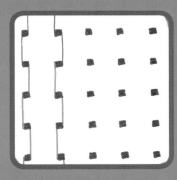

4. Repeat steps 2 and 3 until you reach the bottom of the paper, alternating between the left and right-hand edges.

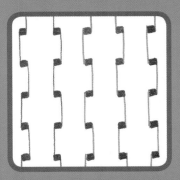

5. Continue working your way down the vertical rows, alternating the lines each time.

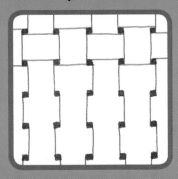

6. Now start drawing lines across the horizontal rows, alternating the lines between the top and bottom edges of the squares.

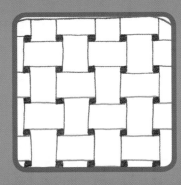

7. Continue adding lines until all of the squares are joined up.

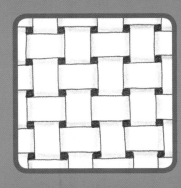

8. Add shading around the edges of the lines to complete the woven effect.

Darting Dragonfly

Dragonflies can dart quickly to and fro, up and down, or even stop and hover. Follow these steps to create your own fantastic flyer with a matching pair of delicately tangled wings.

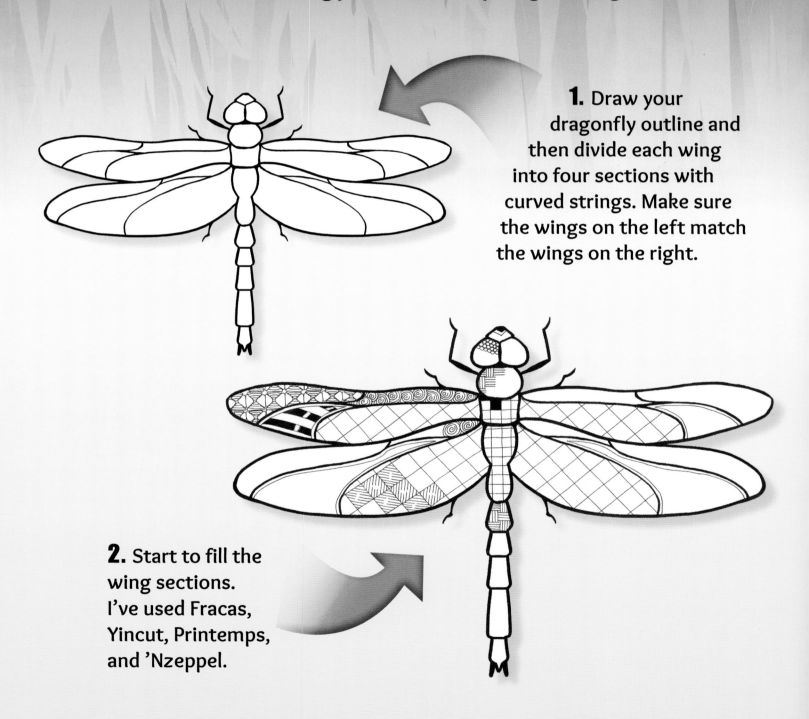

1. Draw your dragonfly outline and then divide each wing into four sections with curved strings. Make sure the wings on the left match the wings on the right.

2. Start to fill the wing sections. I've used Fracas, Yincut, Printemps, and 'Nzeppel.

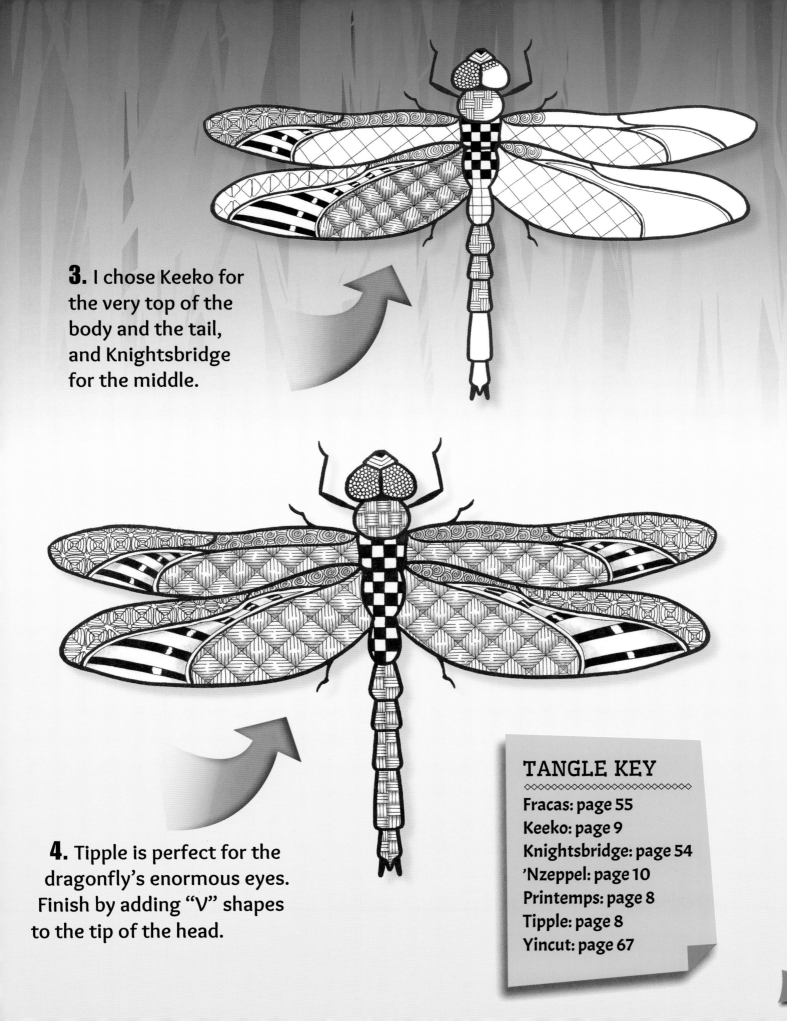

3. I chose Keeko for the very top of the body and the tail, and Knightsbridge for the middle.

4. Tipple is perfect for the dragonfly's enormous eyes. Finish by adding "V" shapes to the tip of the head.

TANGLE KEY

Fracas: page 55
Keeko: page 9
Knightsbridge: page 54
'Nzeppel: page 10
Printemps: page 8
Tipple: page 8
Yincut: page 67

Hurry

Don't rush! Take your time and this tangle of overlapping lines will look awesome on any bug.

1. Start by drawing a pair of parallel lines across the page to make a band. Draw another band in the opposite direction. When you meet the first band, stop drawing and then continue on the other side.

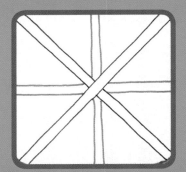

2. Draw a horizontal band and a vertical band across the middle, stopping where you meet another band and continuing on the other side.

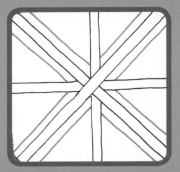

3. Draw lines on either side of the diagonal bands, keeping them an even distance apart.

4. Now add lines on either side of the horizontal and vertical bands.

5. Keep adding diagonal, horizontal, and vertical lines in turn.

6. Continue to add lines until you have filled the space.

7. Add shading around the edge of the tangled area.

Hollibaugh

This random tangle makes a great contrast to rows of regular patterns.

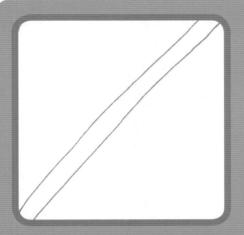

1. Start by drawing a pair of parallel lines across the page to make a band. You can draw the lines in any direction.

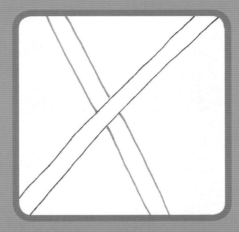

2. Draw another band going in a different direction. When you reach the first band, stop drawing and then continue on the other side.

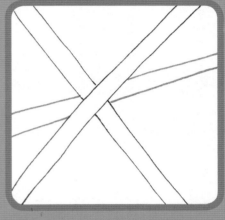

3. Add a further band in a different direction to the first two. Stop when you meet any lines and continue on the other side.

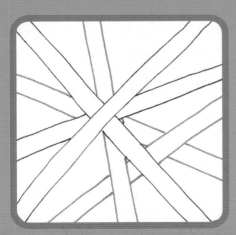

4. Continue to add more bands in different directions until you are happy with the effect.

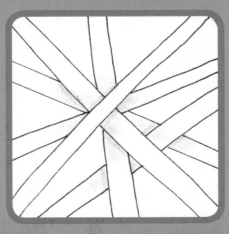

5. Finally, add shading where each band meets another one.

Tangle Tip!
You could fill the gaps between each band with other tangles, such as Tipple, to add extra detail.

Buzzy Bee

In summer, gardens hum with the sound of bees busily collecting nectar. Creating a buzz of your own is easy. Just follow the steps to create this brilliant bee picture!

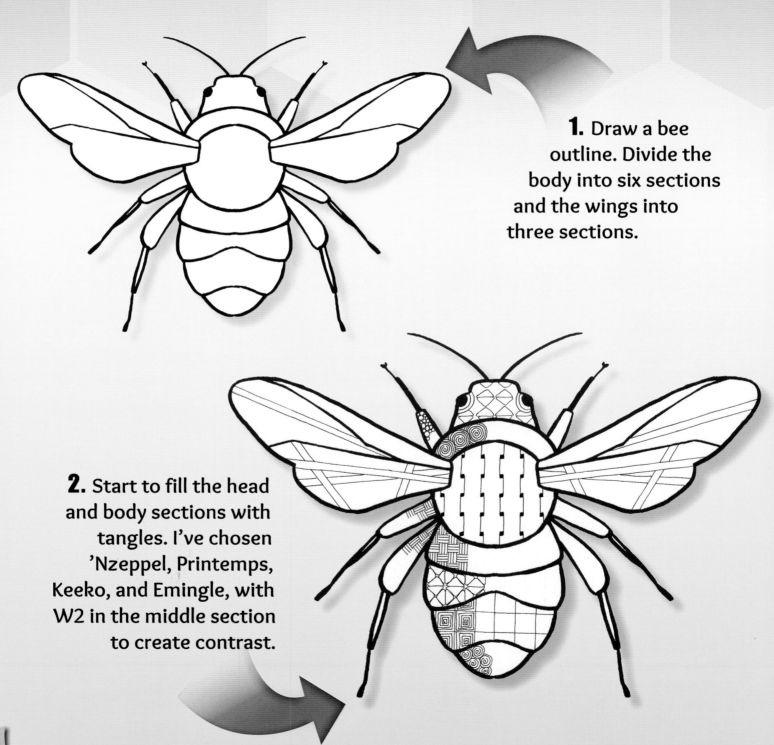

1. Draw a bee outline. Divide the body into six sections and the wings into three sections.

2. Start to fill the head and body sections with tangles. I've chosen 'Nzeppel, Printemps, Keeko, and Emingle, with W2 in the middle section to create contrast.

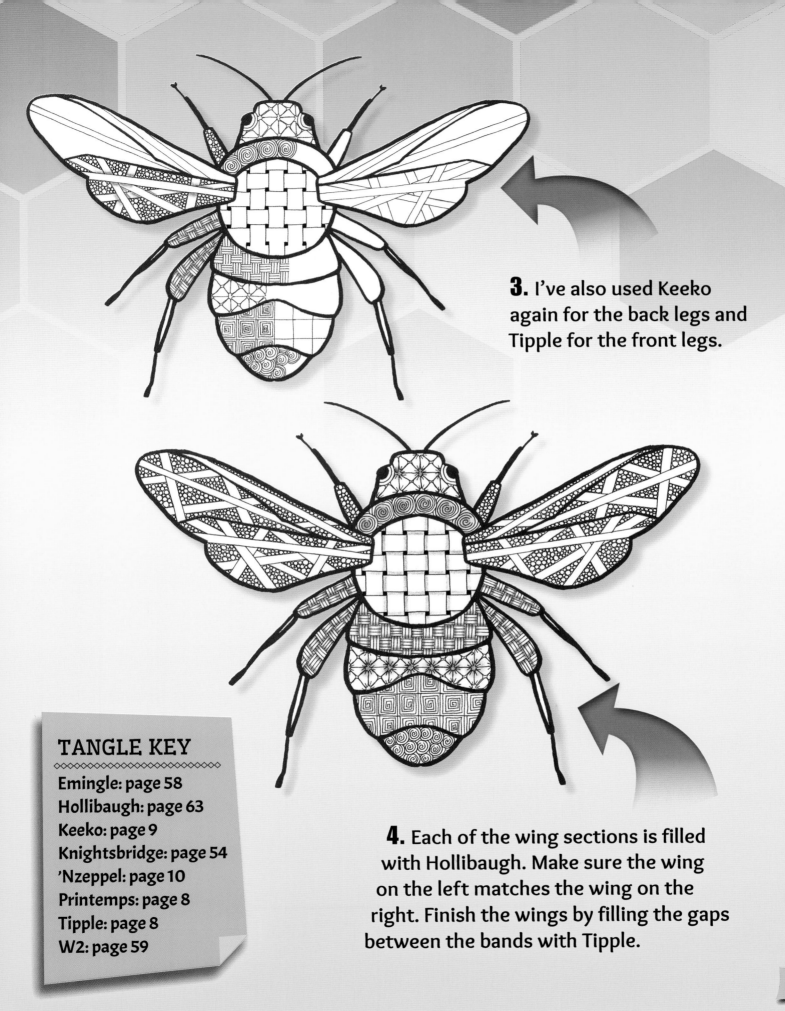

3. I've also used Keeko again for the back legs and Tipple for the front legs.

TANGLE KEY

Emingle: page 58
Hollibaugh: page 63
Keeko: page 9
Knightsbridge: page 54
'Nzeppel: page 10
Printemps: page 8
Tipple: page 8
W2: page 59

4. Each of the wing sections is filled with Hollibaugh. Make sure the wing on the left matches the wing on the right. Finish the wings by filling the gaps between the bands with Tipple.

Jetties

Roll out this tangle of marble-like balls whenever a picture needs some striking spots.

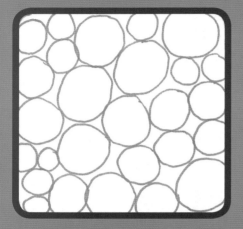

1. Start by drawing a selection of large circles on your paper and then draw some smaller circles in the gaps.

2. On each circle, draw two lines across the middle to form a band and fill them in with your pen. Draw the bands at different angles.

3. Add a line slightly above each band and another line slightly below.

4. Shade with a pencil below each band to finish the tangle off.

Tangle Tip!
Try varying the patterns inside the circles to change the look.

Yincut

This cool, quilted tangle is perfect for giving hard objects a soft, padded effect.

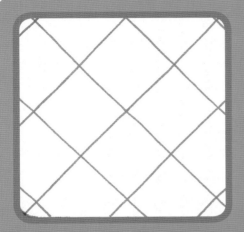

1. Draw evenly spaced diagonal lines going in both directions across your paper to make a grid of diamonds.

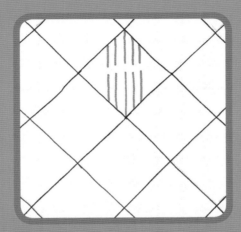

2. In the middle of one of the diamonds, draw 4 or 5 vertical lines, leaving a small gap halfway down.

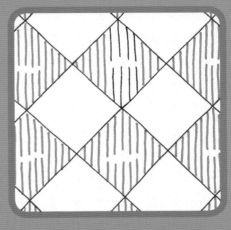

3. Draw more lines on either side to fill the shape, but this time don't leave a gap. Continue filling the diamonds with lines, leaving every other row of diamonds blank.

4. Now fill in all the blank diamonds with horizontal lines. Again, leave a little gap in the lines in the middle.

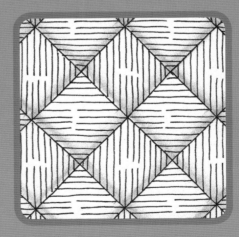

5. Add some pencil shading along the bottom edges of each diamond to complete the tangle.

Beautiful Butterfly

Butterflies are famous for their bright patterns and fluttering flight. Create a pretty butterfly of your own with a pair of beautifully tangled wings.

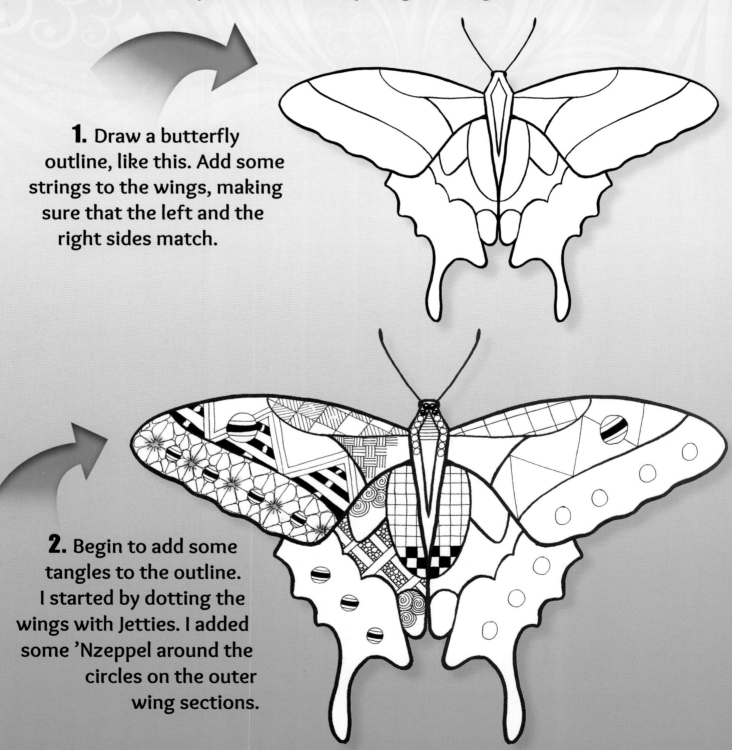

1. Draw a butterfly outline, like this. Add some strings to the wings, making sure that the left and the right sides match.

2. Begin to add some tangles to the outline. I started by dotting the wings with Jetties. I added some 'Nzeppel around the circles on the outer wing sections.

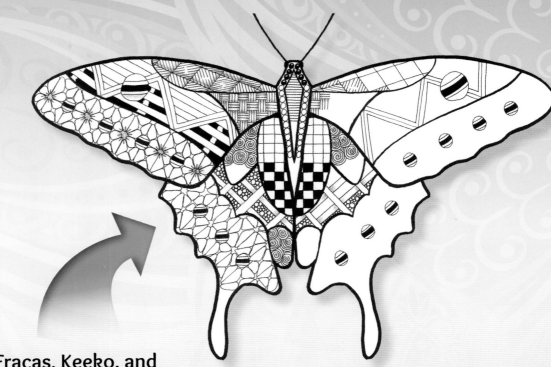

3. I chose Fracas, Keeko, and Yincut for the remaining sections of the upper wings. I've filled the body with some little circles.

4. The inner sections of the lower wings are filled with Knightsbridge, Printemps, and Hollibaugh, with Tipple in the gaps.

Tangle Time!

Use your best tangles to finish these bugs!

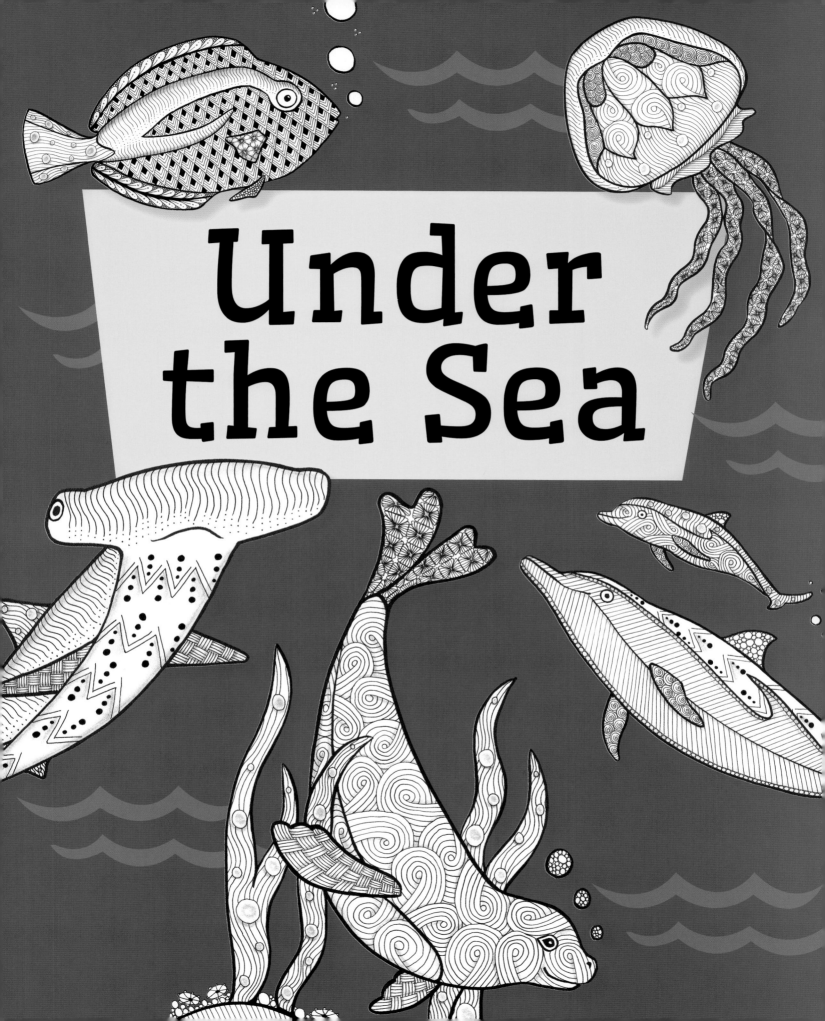

Under the Sea

Cute Seal

A seal's sleek body is perfectly designed for life in the water. Follow these steps to design a super swimmer of your own with some ocean-inspired tangles.

1. Draw the outline of a seal with seaweed and the seabed. Add a string along the seal's tummy.

2. I've used Sand Swirl for the seal's body, 'Nzeppel for its tail, and Keeko for its flippers.

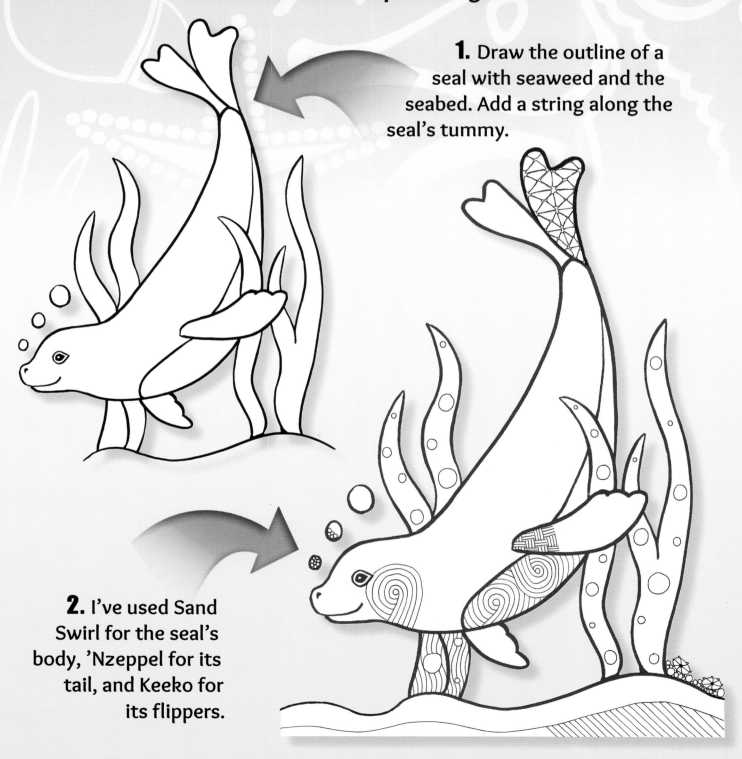

3. I chose Meer for the seabed and Nipa for the seaweed.

TANGLE KEY

Festune: page 87
Keeko: page 9
Meer: page 82
Nipa: page 74
'Nzeppel: page 10
Sand Swirl: page 75
Tipple: page 8

4. Finish the picture by filling the bubbles with Tipple and adding some tangles to the seafloor. I've used Festune here.

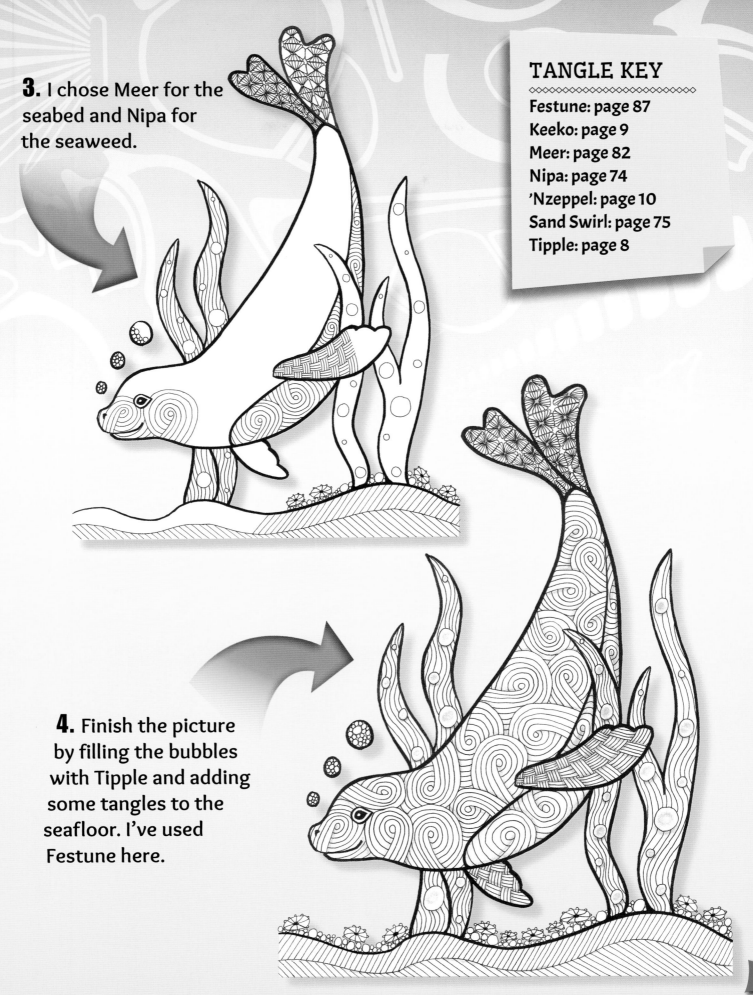

Nipa

This wavy tangle looks like ripples and rising bubbles. It's perfect for any underwater picture!

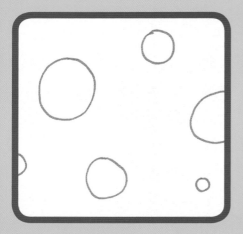

1. Start by drawing some well-spaced, different sized circles across the paper.

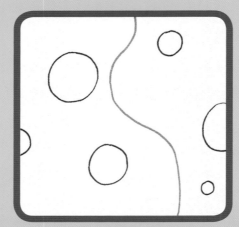

2. Draw a wavy line down the middle of the paper.

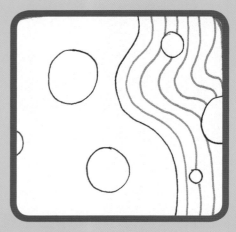

3. Draw more evenly spaced wavy lines on the right, following the shape of the first line. When you reach a circle, stop drawing and continue the line on the other side.

4. Now draw wavy lines on the left of the first line, remembering not to draw through the circles.

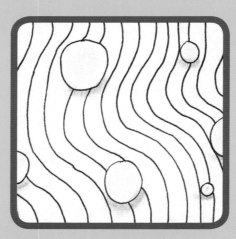

5. Add depth with some pencil shading inside and underneath each circle and then smudge with your finger.

Tangle Tip!
You could fill in a few of the circles with your pen, to vary the look of this tangle.

Sand Swirl

This swirly tangle of crashing waves will bring a sense of fun and energy to almost any marine animal.

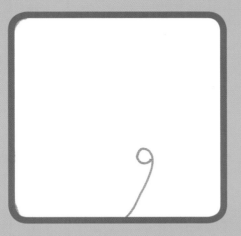

1. Starting at the bottom of the paper, draw a slightly curved line with a circle at the end.

2. Slightly below the circle, draw another curved line (an "aura") around the circle and down to the bottom.

3. Add another aura to start to create a swirl. Then draw more curved lines with circles around the outside of the paper.

4. Continue adding auras to the first swirl until you have about five. Then add more auras to the other lines. When you meet another swirl, stop drawing and continue on the other side.

5. Finish with shading and smudging along the inside of each of the original curved lines.

Tropical Fish

Tropical seas teem with bright fish darting among the coral.
Create this prize tang fish covered in sea-themed tangles
and eye-catching scales.

1. Copy this tang fish with its striped body and fins. Add some bubbles, too.

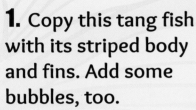

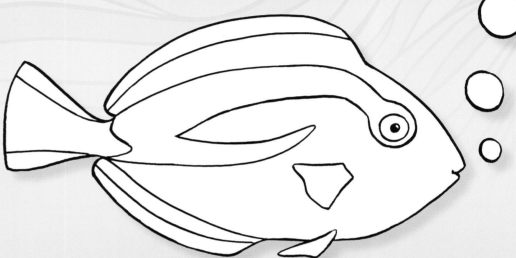

2. Start by choosing a tangle for the fish's body. I chose Flukes for a nice scaly look.

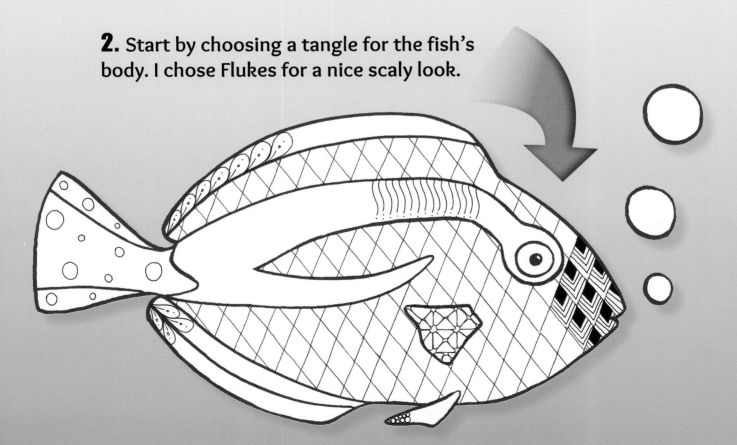

3. Add some more contrasting tangles. I used Flux for the fringes at the top and the bottom of the fish, and 'Nzeppel and Tipple for the fins.

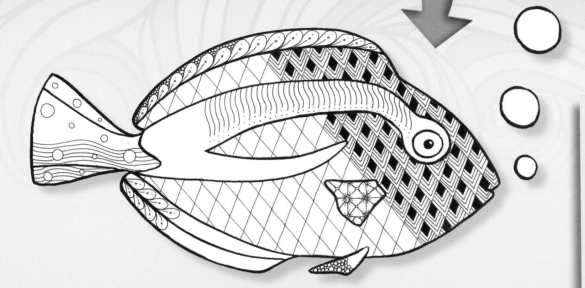

TANGLE KEY

Flukes: page 78
Flux: page 79
Meer: page 82
Nipa: page 74
'Nzeppel: page 10
Tipple: page 8

4. I tangled the tail with Nipa and the middle stripe with Meer. Shade and smudge along this stripe to give the fish a fuller shape.

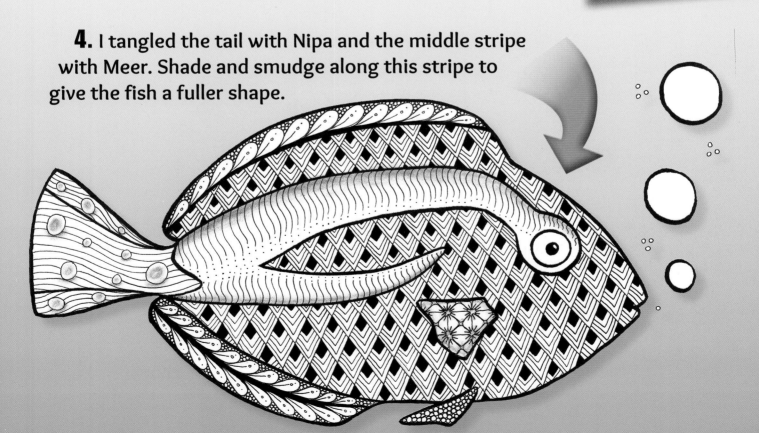

Flukes

The overlapping squares in this tangle make a striking set of scales for any kind of fish.

1. Start by drawing diagonal lines across your paper.

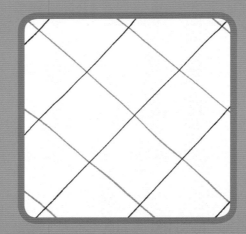

2. Draw more diagonal lines in the opposite direction to form a grid of diamonds.

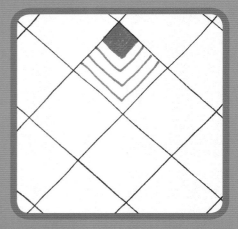

3. Draw a small diamond in the top of one of the diamonds and use your pen to fill it in. Then add three evenly spaced "Vs" below the little diamond to fill the shape.

4. Repeat this pattern in each diamond until they are all filled.

5. Your tangle is complete!

Flux

I often dot Flux around the seafloor for perfect seaweed and pebbles.

1. Start by drawing a leaf shape. Decorate the shape by drawing a line from the bottom to the middle and adding a few dots above it.

2. Draw more leaf shapes around the first one, adding lines and dots inside them all.

3. Fill the space around the shapes with Tipple (page 8).

Tangle Tip!

Make your Flux shape tall so it looks like strands of seaweed swaying in the water.

Playful Dolphins

Dolphins love to leap and splash as they speed through the water. Follow these steps to create a mother and baby dolphin with playful tangles to match their mood.

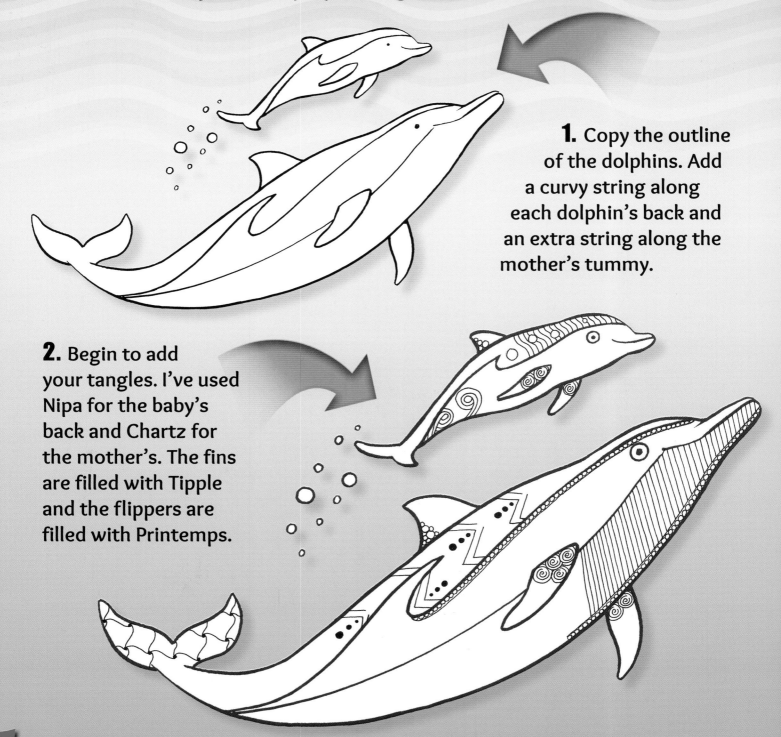

1. Copy the outline of the dolphins. Add a curvy string along each dolphin's back and an extra string along the mother's tummy.

2. Begin to add your tangles. I've used Nipa for the baby's back and Chartz for the mother's. The fins are filled with Tipple and the flippers are filled with Printemps.

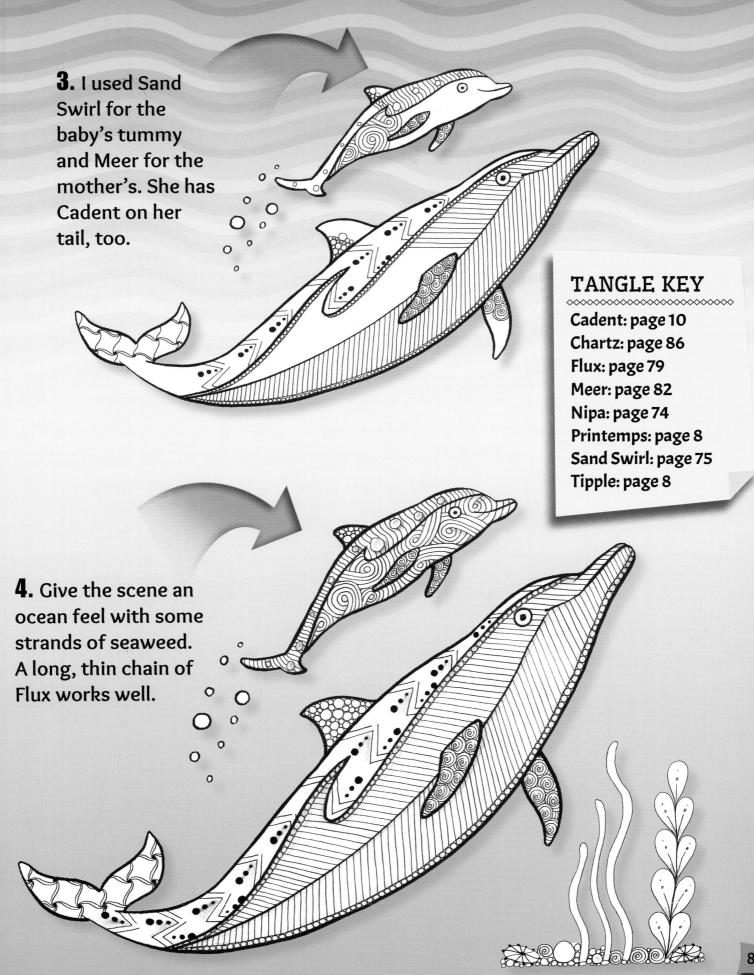

3. I used Sand Swirl for the baby's tummy and Meer for the mother's. She has Cadent on her tail, too.

TANGLE KEY

Cadent: page 10
Chartz: page 86
Flux: page 79
Meer: page 82
Nipa: page 74
Printemps: page 8
Sand Swirl: page 75
Tipple: page 8

4. Give the scene an ocean feel with some strands of seaweed. A long, thin chain of Flux works well.

Meer

This flowing tangle suggests ocean waves
and strings of pearls.

1. Start by drawing two pairs of lines leaving a space in the middle.

2. Draw a row of small, closely packed circles along the outer lines. Draw a wavy line through the middle of the tangle.

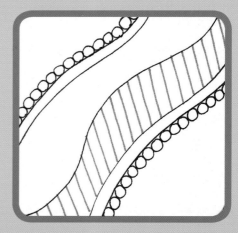

3. Fill the area on the right of the wavy line with evenly spaced diagonal lines.

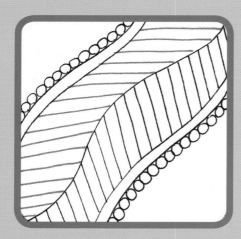

4. Now repeat on the other side of the wavy line with lines going in the opposite direction.

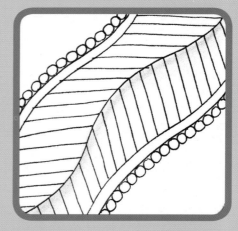

5. Add pencil shading below the wavy line and smudge with your finger to finish.

Msst

This delicate tangle is like threads of seaweed swaying in the water.

1. Start by drawing a wavy line at the top of your paper.

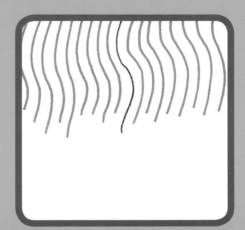

2. Add more evenly spaced lines on either side. You can make the lines different lengths, but they should all follow the shape of the first line.

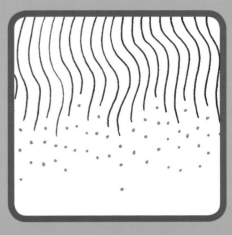

3. Add 3 or 4 dots below each wavy line.

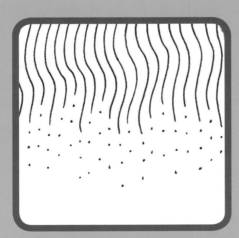

4. Shade and smudge across the middle of the wavy lines.

Tangle Tip!
Draw the dots at random below each wavy line to create a natural look.

Wobbly Jellyfish

Jellyfish are not good swimmers, so they just drift along on the ocean currents. Tangle a wobbly jellyfish of your own with wonderful trailing tentacles.

1. Draw the outline of your jellyfish with four wavy tentacles. Add strings for the tangles, as shown.

2. Start to fill the areas between the strings. I'm using Msst for the outer section of the jellyfish and Printemps for the four smallest inner sections.

3. The large petal-shaped sections are filled with Sand Swirl and the bottom section is filled with Nipa.

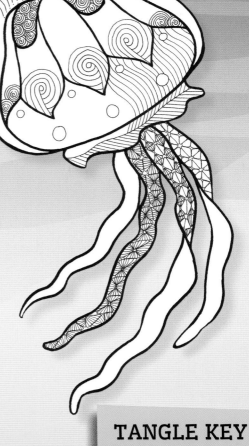

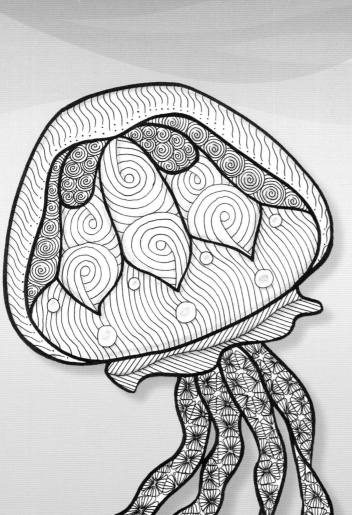

TANGLE KEY

Meer: page 82
Msst: page 83
Nipa: page 74
'Nzeppel: page 10
Printemps: page 8
Sand Swirl: page 75

4. I've used Meer without the circles for the frill at the bottom of the jellyfish's body and 'Nzeppel for the tentacles.

Chartz

Give your pictures an extra edge with this spiky, spotty tangle.

1. Draw a diagonal zigzag across the page.

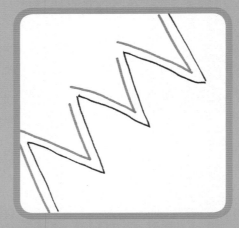

2. Draw a "V" shape inside each "V" of the zigzag, leaving a slight gap at the top.

3. Draw a small dot at the deepest point of the first "V" and fill it in with your pen. Add three more dots in a row, making each one slightly larger.

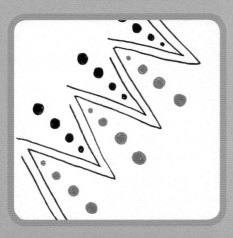

4. Now add rows of dots on the other side of the zigzag.

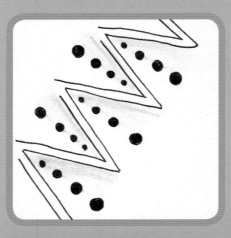

5. To finish, add some pencil shading on the right-hand side of each "V".

Tangle Tip!
This tangle would work really well for a shark picture. The zigzags hint at its razor-sharp teeth!

Festune

This beach-inspired tangle could be a cluster of barnacles, sea urchins, or tiny shells.

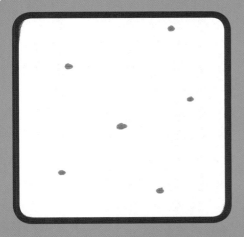

1. Start by drawing big dots across the paper.

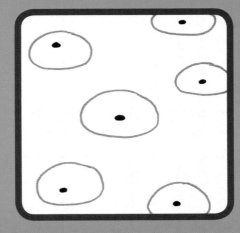

2. Draw a sideways oval around each dot.

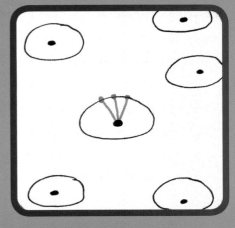

3. On one oval, draw a slightly curved line from the dot in the middle to the the outside of the shape. Finish it with a dot. Repeat all the way around the oval.

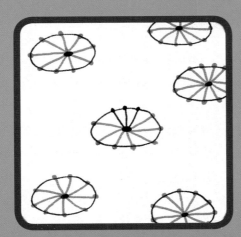

4. Continue until you have drawn lines on every oval. Draw as many lines as you like, making sure they are evenly spaced.

5. Fill the space with Festune for a busy look. Add pencil shading inside each oval shape to finish.

Hammerhead Shark

Hammerhead sharks sweep through the water, scanning the ocean with their wide-set eyes. Design your own deep-sea hunter covered with striking tangles.

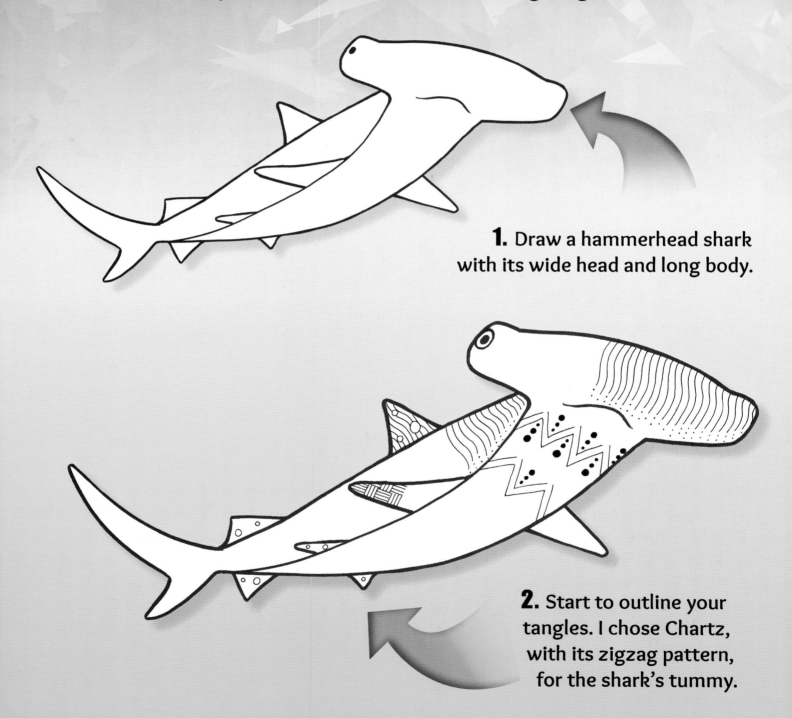

1. Draw a hammerhead shark with its wide head and long body.

2. Start to outline your tangles. I chose Chartz, with its zigzag pattern, for the shark's tummy.

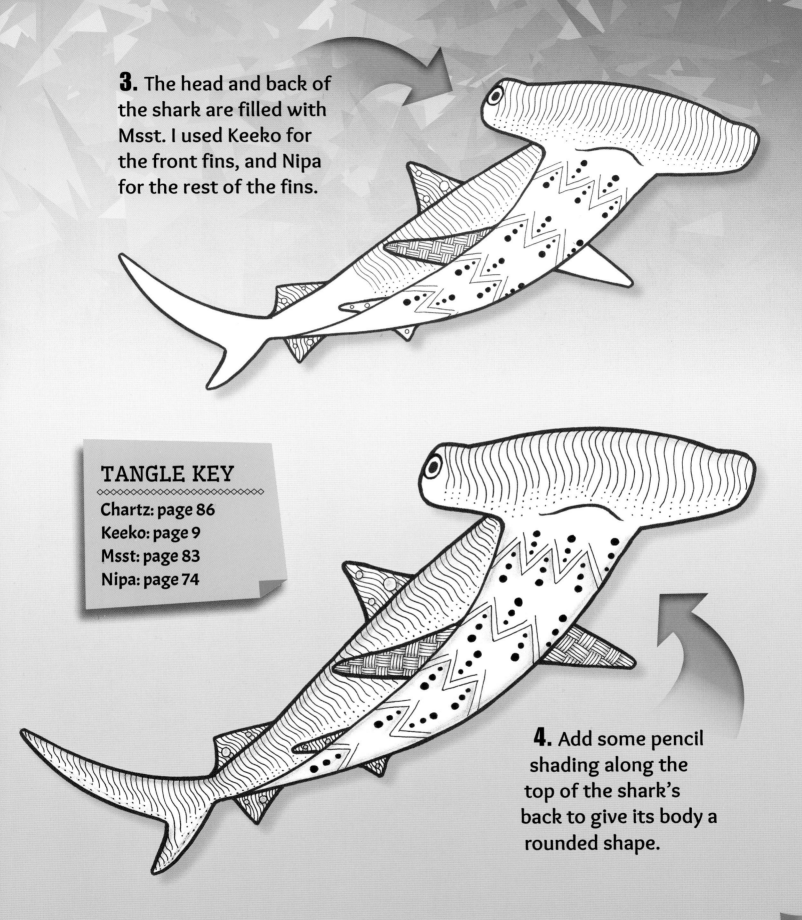

3. The head and back of the shark are filled with Msst. I used Keeko for the front fins, and Nipa for the rest of the fins.

TANGLE KEY

Chartz: page 86
Keeko: page 9
Msst: page 83
Nipa: page 74

4. Add some pencil shading along the top of the shark's back to give its body a rounded shape.

Tangle Time!

Use some marine-themed tangles to complete these ocean creatures.

Holidays

Christmas Tree

Christmas is nearly here and it's time to decorate the tree! Draw this fine pine, hang festive tangles on its branches, and top it off with a sparkling star.

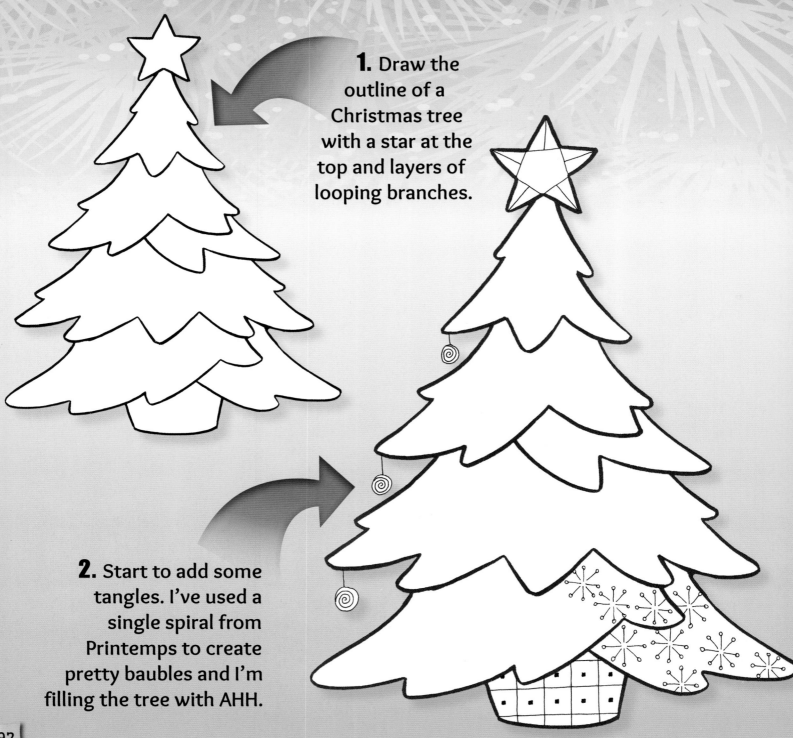

1. Draw the outline of a Christmas tree with a star at the top and layers of looping branches.

2. Start to add some tangles. I've used a single spiral from Printemps to create pretty baubles and I'm filling the tree with AHH.

TANGLE KEY
◇◇◇◇◇◇◇◇◇◇◇◇◇◇◇◇◇◇◇◇◇◇
AHH: page 94
'Nzeppel: page 10
Printemps: page 8
Stoic: page 95

3. Stoic gives the basket underneath the tree a nice woven effect.

4. For the star, I've used a single flower of 'Nzeppel for the middle, and added some lines on each point to make it look 3D.

AHH

This flashy tangle adds a burst of festivity to any Christmas picture.

1. Draw two vertical lines, leaving a gap in the middle.

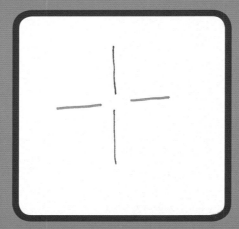

2. Draw two horizontal lines to make a cross shape, leaving a gap in the middle.

3. Add four more lines in an "X" shape, leaving a gap in the middle.

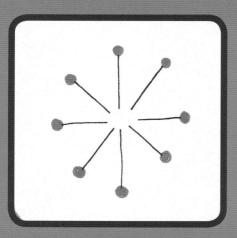

4. Add a circle at the end of each line and use your pen to fill them in.

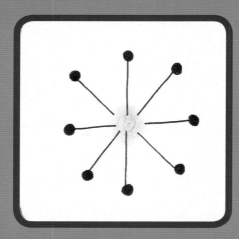

5. Add a smudge of pencil to the gap in the middle.

Tangle Tip!
The smudge in the middle of AHH really adds some twinkle. This tangle would look great on a homemade Christmas card!

Stoic

Wrap this woven tangle around any shape for a brilliant basket effect.

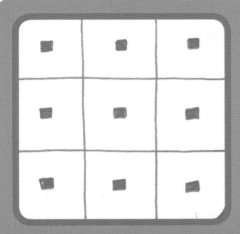

1. Divide the paper into a grid of squares by drawing vertical and horizontal lines. Draw a small square in the middle of each square and fill it in with your pen.

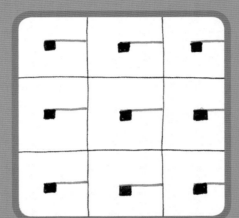

2. Draw a line from the top edge of every small square to meet the line on the right.

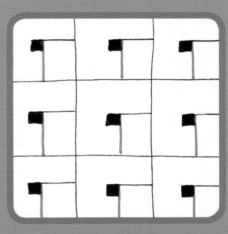

3. Now draw a line from the right edge of every small square to meet the line below.

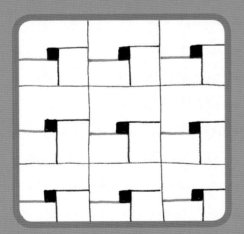

4. Continue by drawing a line from the bottom edge of every small square to meet the line on the left.

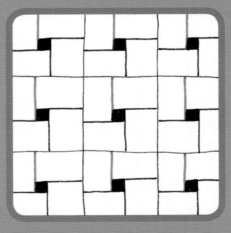

5. Finish the tangle by drawing a line from the left edge of every small square to meet the line above.

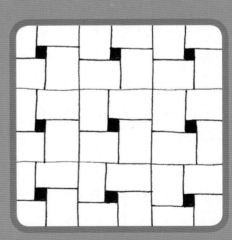

6. Your pretty tangle is complete!

Peaceful Angel

This beautiful angel brings a message of peace and goodwill at Christmas time. Follow these steps to create your own heavenly angel with a hovering halo and wonderfully tangled wings.

1. Draw the outline of an angel. Add strings to her dress and layers of strings on her wings, making sure both wings match.

2. Begin to add your tangles. I've gone for a square theme on the wings, with Keeko at the top, Bales in the middle, and Eye-wa at the bottom.

3. I've used Aztec for the top of the dress and Eke for the flowing skirt.

TANGLE KEY

Aztec: page 103
Bales: page 9
Eke: page 99
Eye-wa: page 98
Keeko: page 9
Printemps: page 8

4. Finish by filling the halo. I've gone for Printemps here. I added shading to the halo and the top of the wings, too.

Eye-wa

Look at this eye-popping pattern for long enough and you might see it staring back at you!

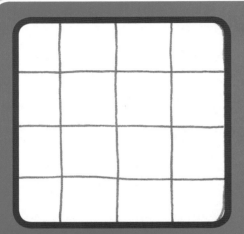

1. Start by drawing vertical and horizontal lines over the paper to make a grid.

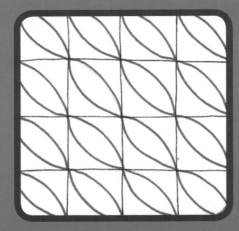

2. In each square, draw a pointed petal shape from top left to bottom right.

3. Use your pen to fill in the spaces on either side of the petal shapes in every other square.

4. Now fill in the petal shape in every square that has not been shaded.

5. Your jazzy tangle is finished!

Tangle Tip!

Eye-wa and Eke are good tangles to use to fill up a large space. You could add them to gift-wrap, to give your presents a personal touch.

Eke

This twirly tangle looks like pretty party streamers
or strings of festive fairy lights.

1. Start by drawing a loop that looks like an "e" with a long tail.

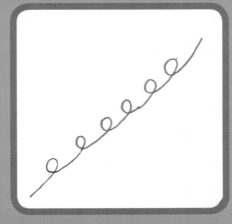

2. Repeat with a long row of joined up loops.

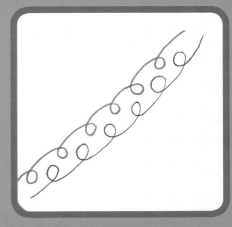

3. Now draw a row of upside-down loops opposite the first row. Make the circles in these loops sit in the spaces between the loops opposite.

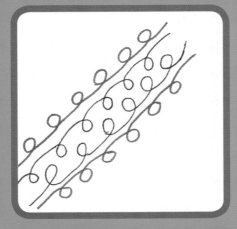

4. Repeat with rows of loops on either side, alternating the way the loops face each time.

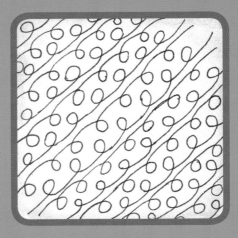

5. Continue adding loops until you have filled the space. Add some shading and smudge to finish.

Halloween Pumpkin

You're in for a spooky treat this Halloween! Use a few Zentangle tricks to craft this patterned pumpkin with slanted eyes and a ghoulish grin.

1. Draw a simple pumpkin outline with curved lines coming from the stalk in the middle.

2. Choose a really bold tangle for the pumpkin itself. I've used Stricles. Start to draw in the eyes as well.

3. I used 'Nzeppel for the leaves and added short lines along the edge of the pumpkin stalk for shading.

TANGLE KEY
◇◇◇◇◇◇◇◇◇◇◇◇◇◇◇◇◇◇◇◇◇◇◇
'Nzeppel: page 10
Stricles: page 102

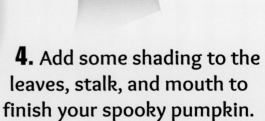

4. Add some shading to the leaves, stalk, and mouth to finish your spooky pumpkin.

Stricles

This bendy, dotty tangle knocks spots off ordinary stripes.

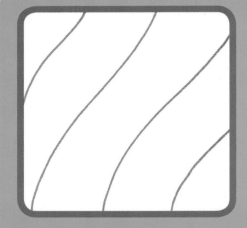

1. Draw wavy lines at an angle across the paper.

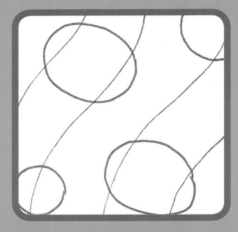

2. Add big circles overlapping one or two of the wavy lines.

3. Using your pen, shade between every other pair of lines to make stripes. Don't shade inside the circles.

4. Now fill in the part of each circle that does not overlap one of the shaded stripes.

5. Your tangle is finished!

Aztec

Use this tangle as a border around the edge of an outline, or to neatly fill a narrow space.

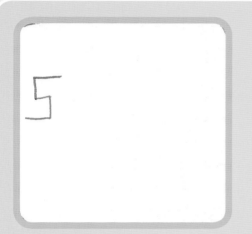

1. Draw a shape a bit like an "S", but with straight lines instead of curves.

2. Add a straight line at either end of your "S" shape.

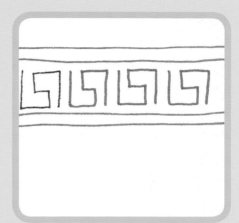

3. Add a row of these shapes and draw two straight lines above and below the row.

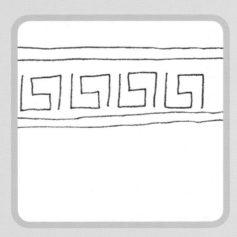

4. Your tangle is complete!

Tangle Tip!

You don't have to add the band of lines above the shapes. Have a look at how I've used Aztec on the Angel (pages 96-97).

Easter Chick

Easter is a time for chicks, chocolates, and brightly painted eggs. Make a cracking start to your celebration with this newly hatched Zentangle chick.

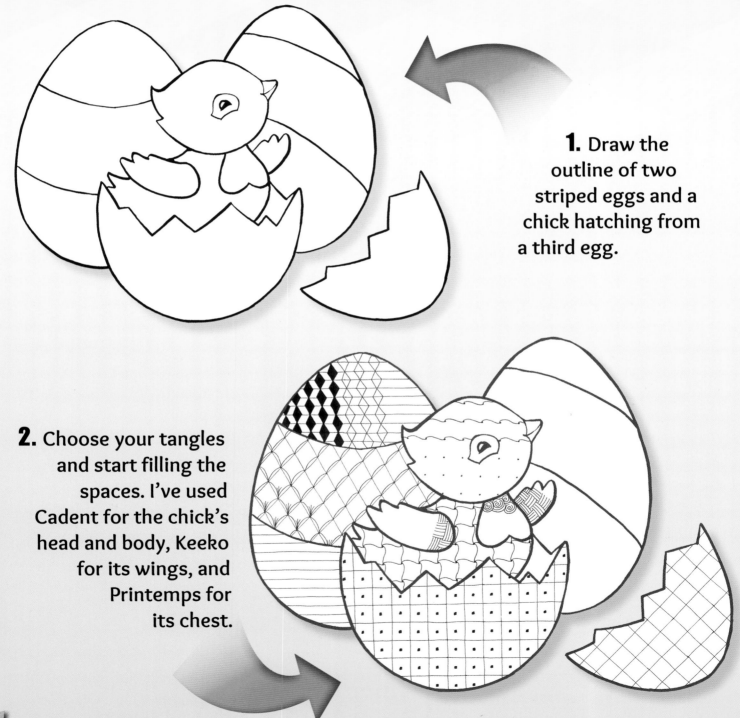

1. Draw the outline of two striped eggs and a chick hatching from a third egg.

2. Choose your tangles and start filling the spaces. I've used Cadent for the chick's head and body, Keeko for its wings, and Printemps for its chest.

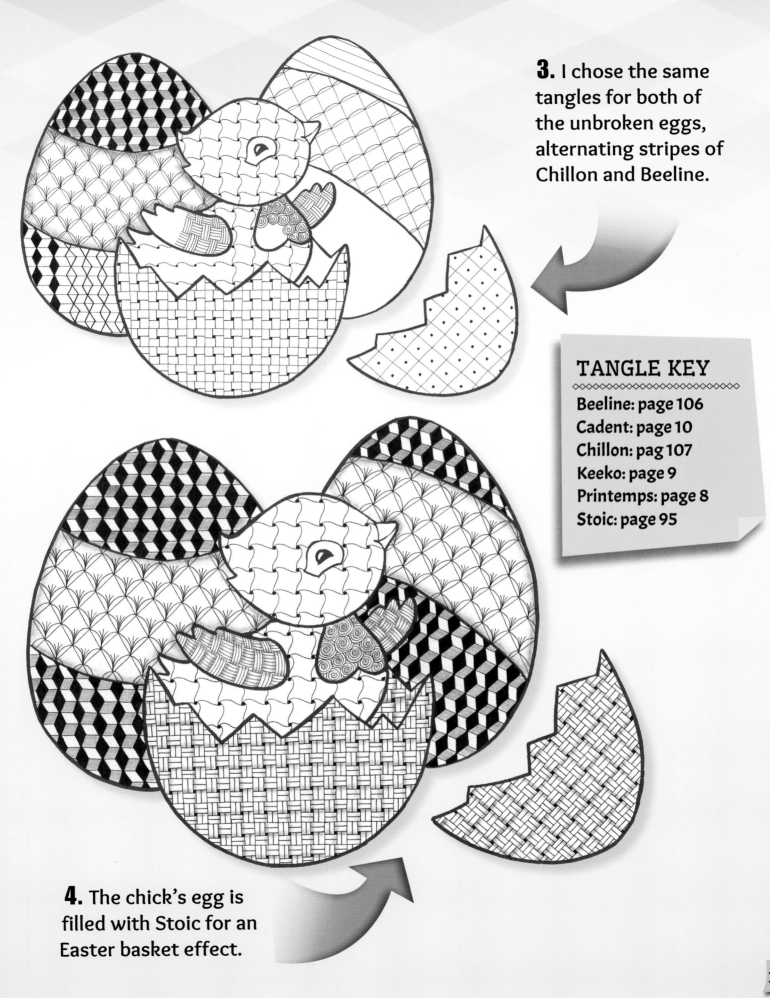

3. I chose the same tangles for both of the unbroken eggs, alternating stripes of Chillon and Beeline.

TANGLE KEY

Beeline: page 106
Cadent: page 10
Chillon: pag 107
Keeko: page 9
Printemps: page 8
Stoic: page 95

4. The chick's egg is filled with Stoic for an Easter basket effect.

Beeline

Build some Beeline into your pictures and add some simple shading to give a flat surface a blocky, 3D effect.

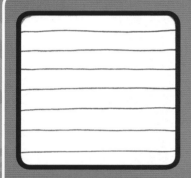

1. Begin by drawing evenly spaced horizontal lines across the page.

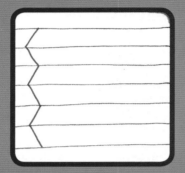

2. Starting in the top left, draw a vertical zigzag line down the page. Each point in the zigzag must meet a horizontal line.

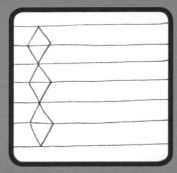

3. Now draw a zigzag line opposite the first one. Draw this zigzag facing the other way to form a row of diamonds.

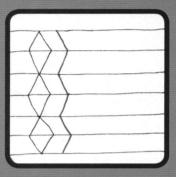

4. Draw another zigzag following the outline of the previous row.

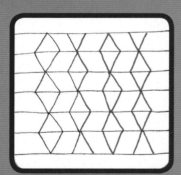

5. Repeat steps 2 to 4 until the area is filled with rows of diamonds.

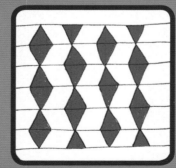

6. Fill in all of the triangle and diamond shapes with your pen.

7. Shade between the horizontal lines in every other row to finish the tangle.

Chillon

The soft waves and cushioning curves of this relaxed tangle make it really easy on the eye.

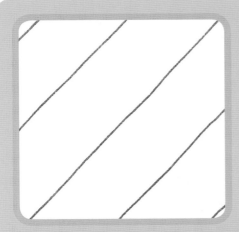

1. Draw evenly spaced diagonal lines across the paper.

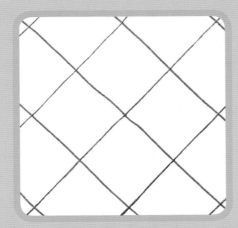

2. Draw diagonal lines in the opposite direction to make a grid of squares.

3. Draw bumps along the tops of all the diagonal lines going one way. Each bump should start and end at the corner of a square.

4. To finish, draw bumps along the tops of the diagonal lines going in the other direction.

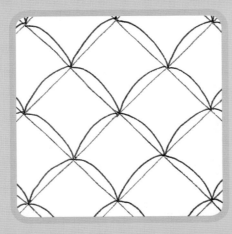

5. Your pretty, bumpy tangle is ready!

Tangle Tip!
You could add extra detail where the lines cross, to vary the look. Have a look at how I've used Chillon on page 105!

Tangle Time!

Use some festive tangles to complete this fun scene.

Fantasy Worlds

Magical Unicorn

Use tangles and plenty of imagination to turn this normally pure white creature into a prancing, patterned unicorn.

1. Start by drawing the outline of your unicorn. Add strings on its back for your tangles.

2. I chose Vega as the main tangle for the unicorn, drawing the lines at different angles for the head, neck, legs, and body.

3. I filled in the areas between the stripes in Vega for a really dramatic effect.

TANGLE KEY

Finery: page 117
Keeko: page 9
Printemps: page 8
Vega: page 112

4. I've used Finery for the unicorn's swishing mane and tail, Printemps for its swirly horn, and Keeko for its hooves.

Vega

This crisscross tangle creates a lovely texture for the fur or scales on your magical creatures.

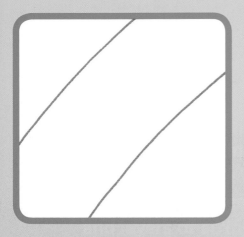

1. Draw two widely spaced curved lines diagonally across the page.

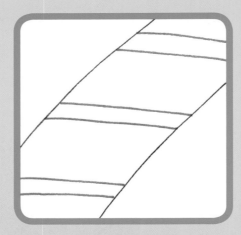

2. Now add pairs of diagonal lines between the curved lines.

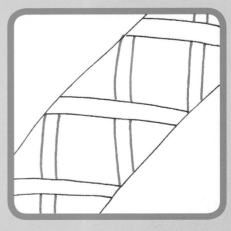

3. Add more pairs of diagonal lines going in the opposite direction. Stop drawing when you reach a line and continue on the other side.

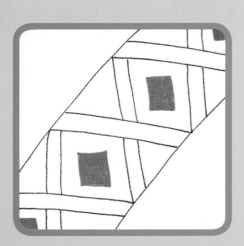

4. Draw a small diamond in the middle of each diamond shaped space and fill it in with your pen.

5. Now draw triangles in each of the triangular spaces and fill these in to finish the tangle.

6. Your tangle is complete! You can make the filled in shapes bigger if you like. Look at how I've used it on the unicorn (page 111).

Crescent Moon

With its dark dots and layers of rings, this tangle is perfect for a pair of beautiful wings.

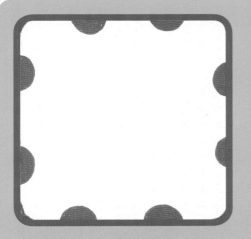

1. Draw small semicircles around the edge of the area and fill them in.

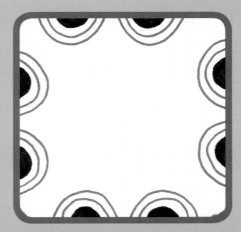

2. Draw two arches, called "auras", around each semicircle.

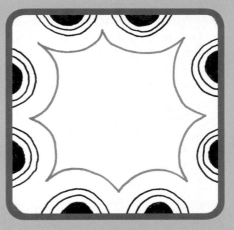

3. Leave a gap and draw joined up arches that follow the shape of the auras, but do not reach the edge of the tangle area.

4. Repeat this pattern, getting smaller each time, until you reach the middle.

5. Draw pencil lines through the points of the joined up arches and smudge for a 3D effect.

Tangle Tip!
Change the look of this tangle by using different shapes for the auras.

Mystical Dragon

Dragons are usually scary, scaly creatures that breathe fire, but you can tangle a magnificent beast of your own with curly spines, spotty wings, and wonderful woven claws!

1. Draw the outline of a seated dragon. Add strings on the neck and at the top of the legs.

2. Choose your tangles and start to fill in the different areas. I've used Crescent Moon for the wings and the tip of the tail and Finery for the tail itself.

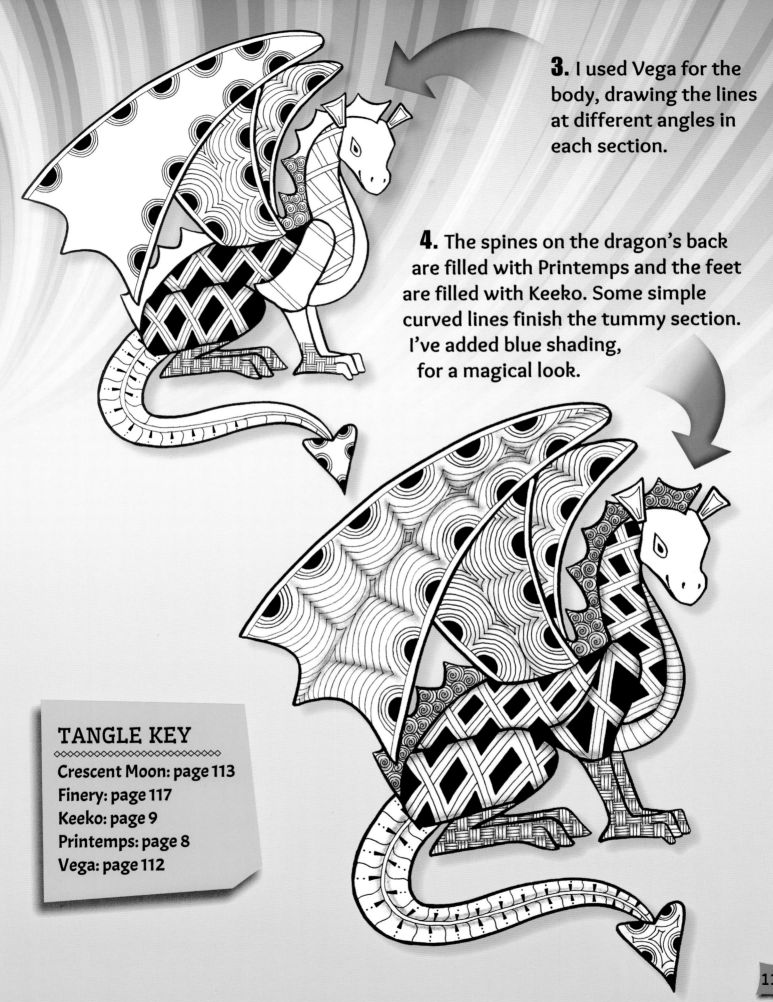

3. I used Vega for the body, drawing the lines at different angles in each section.

4. The spines on the dragon's back are filled with Printemps and the feet are filled with Keeko. Some simple curved lines finish the tummy section. I've added blue shading, for a magical look.

TANGLE KEY

Crescent Moon: page 113
Finery: page 117
Keeko: page 9
Printemps: page 8
Vega: page 112

Jonqual

This dramatic 3D tangle will bring your fantasy creatures to life.

1. Draw evenly spaced diagonal lines across the paper.

2. Draw a zigzag line in the opposite direction across the diagonals.

3. Add evenly spaced zigzags following the shape of the first one. Starting in the second row, fill in every other rectangle with your pen.

4. Continue filling in every other rectangle in every other row until you have finished.

Tangle Tip!
Experiment with the fills or shape of your grid to change the look.

Finery

Use this delicate tangle for a flowing effect on animals' manes and tails.

1. Draw three pairs of diagonal lines across the paper to make bands.

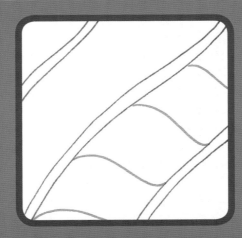

2. Add evenly spaced curved lines between the middle and right-hand bands. Each curved line looks like a stretched back-to-front "S".

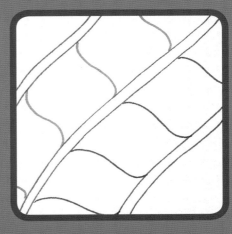

3. Now add curved lines between the middle and left-hand bands going in the opposite direction.

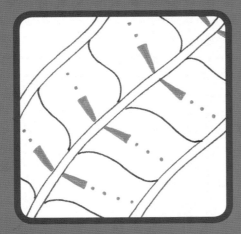

4. Draw narrow triangles between each pair of curved lines on either side of the middle band. Fill in the triangles and add some dots leading to the outer bands.

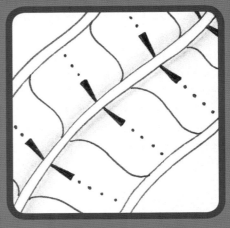

5. Shade and smudge on either side of the middle band to finish.

Beautiful Phoenix

The phoenix is a mythical bird that is said to live for hundreds of years. Create your own Zentangle-inspired version, with wonderful outstretched wings and cleverly tangled tail feathers.

1. Draw a phoenix with four long tail feathers and two sections on each wing.

2. Begin to outline the tangles on the wings. I chose Jonqual for the main section and Tortuca for the inner wing.

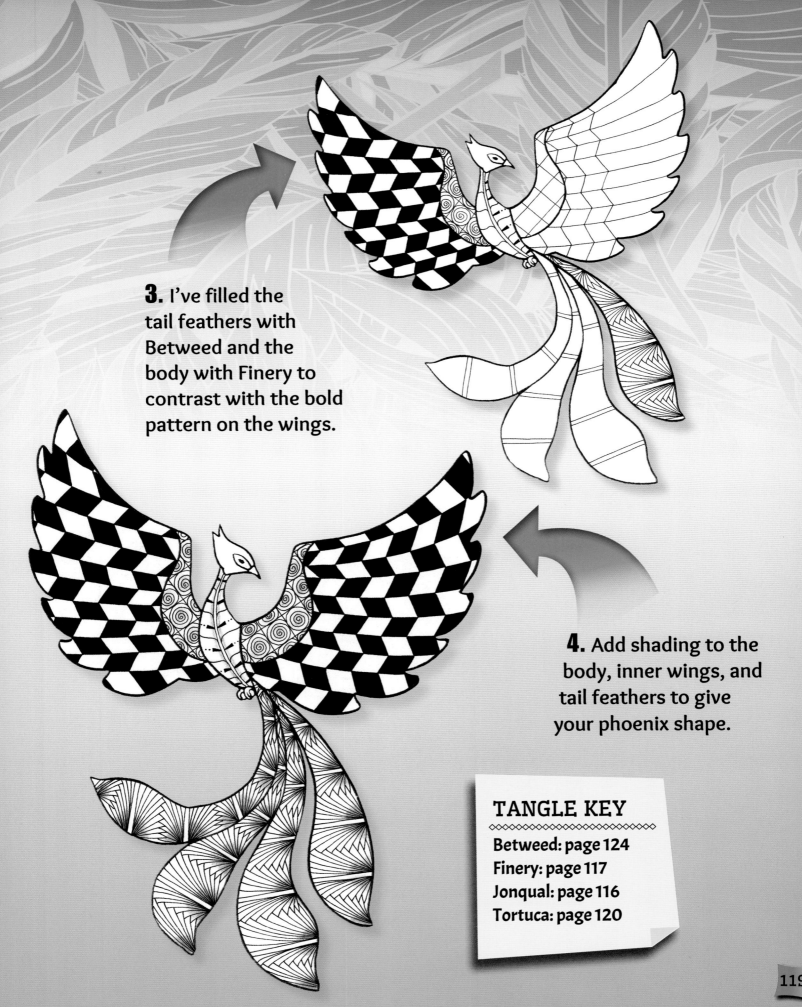

3. I've filled the tail feathers with Betweed and the body with Finery to contrast with the bold pattern on the wings.

4. Add shading to the body, inner wings, and tail feathers to give your phoenix shape.

TANGLE KEY

Betweed: page 124
Finery: page 117
Jonqual: page 116
Tortuca: page 120

Tortuca

This grid of neat and tidy spirals is great for creating curly fur, or for adding a pretty floral pattern.

1. Draw evenly spaced diagonal lines across the paper.

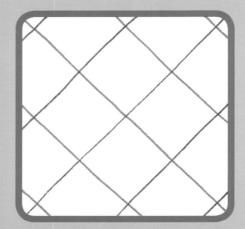

2. Add more diagonal lines in the opposite direction to form a grid of squares.

3. Draw a spiral inside a square, starting at the edge and working your way into the middle.

4. Fill every square with a spiral, always starting at the same place in each square.

5. Your pretty, spiral tangle is ready!

Tangle Tip!
Change the look of Tortuca by adding shading, or by filling in the gaps between the spirals with your pen.

Huggins

Simply join the dots to reveal a totally brilliant basket weave tangle!

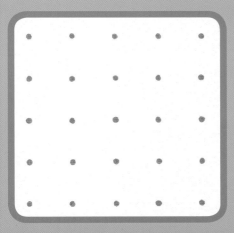

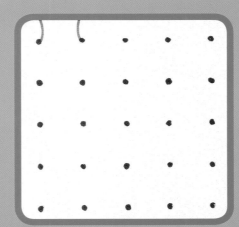

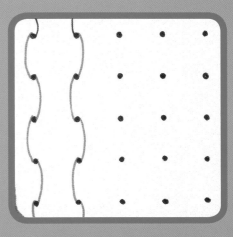

1. Begin by drawing a grid of small, evenly spaced dots.

2. Starting in the top left, draw small curve from the top of the paper to the first dot, as shown. Then draw another small curve from the top of the paper to the second dot.

3. Draw curved lines to the dots below that go in the opposite direction to the ones above. Continue to add more curves down the paper, always alternating their direction.

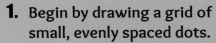

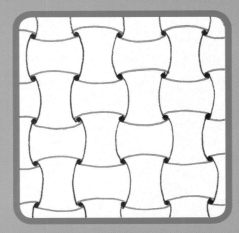

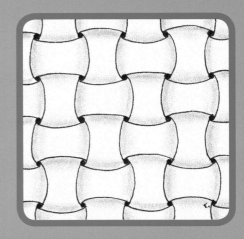

4. Repeat this pattern to fill every vertical row.

5. Now draw pairs of curves in the same way on the horizontal rows.

6. Add shading above and below every horizontal curve to finish.

Ice Queen

Use tangles with sharp points and crisp edges to create the perfect frosty gown for this beautiful ice queen as she sweeps through her frozen palace.

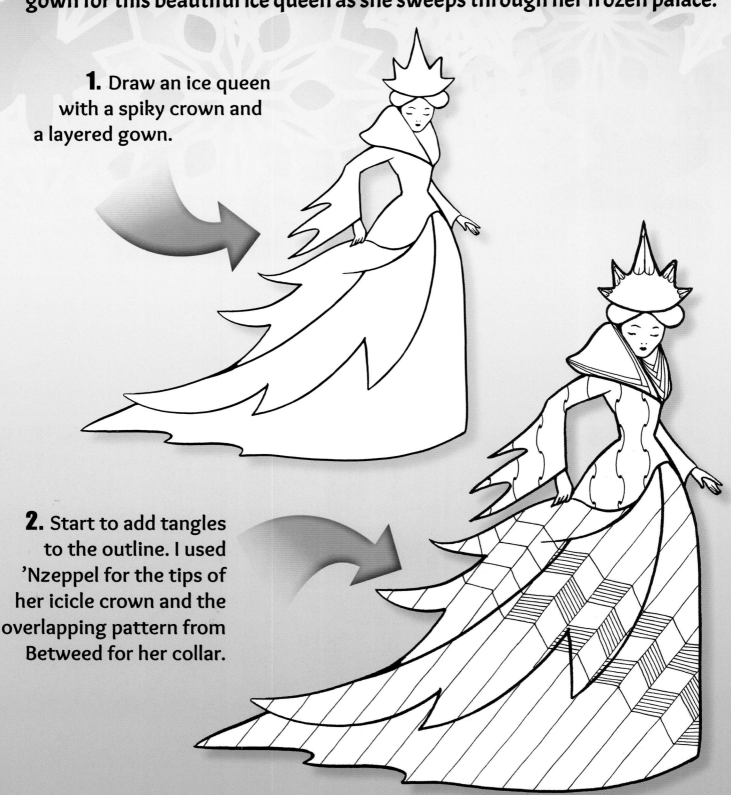

1. Draw an ice queen with a spiky crown and a layered gown.

2. Start to add tangles to the outline. I used 'Nzeppel for the tips of her icicle crown and the overlapping pattern from Betweed for her collar.

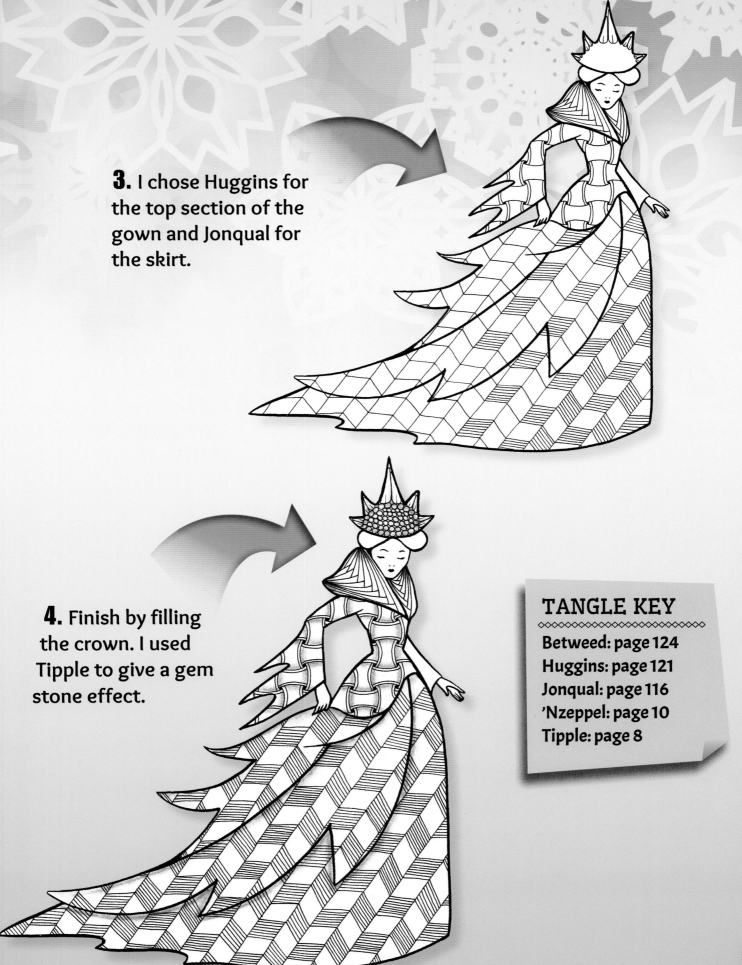

3. I chose Huggins for the top section of the gown and Jonqual for the skirt.

4. Finish by filling the crown. I used Tipple to give a gem stone effect.

TANGLE KEY

Betweed: page 124
Huggins: page 121
Jonqual: page 116
'Nzeppel: page 10
Tipple: page 8

Betweed

This tangle of overlapping layers works perfectly in triangular spaces.

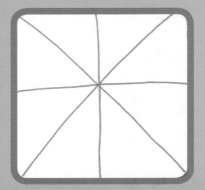

1. Start by drawing an "X" across the paper, and then draw a cross on top to make the pattern shown.

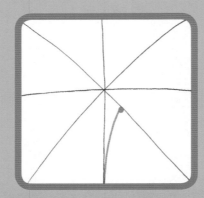

2. In one of the sections, draw a line from the bottom left-hand corner that curves over to the right. When it touches the right-hand line, add a small dot.

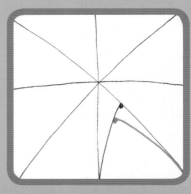

3. Now draw a line that curves in the opposite direction, from the bottom right-hand corner and finishes further down the first curved line. Add a dot to the end of it.

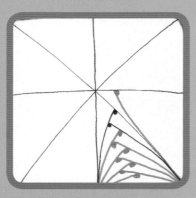

4. Repeat steps 2 and 3, adding curved lines and alternating from left to right until this section is full. Then move on to the next section, always starting in the left-hand corner.

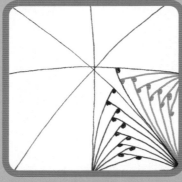

5. Repeat steps 2 to 4 until the second section is full.

6. Complete each section in the same way, always starting in the bottom left-hand corner.

7. Add shading at the points where all the lines meet to complete the tangle.

Daviso

Bring a touch of magic to your fantasy pictures with
this stunning star-spangled tangle!

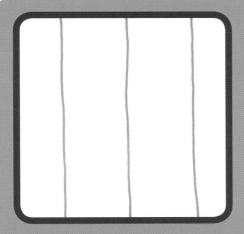

1. Draw evenly spaced vertical lines across the paper.

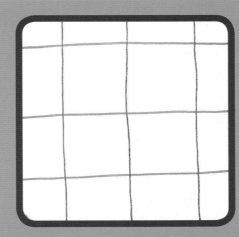

2. Add horizontal lines to form a grid.

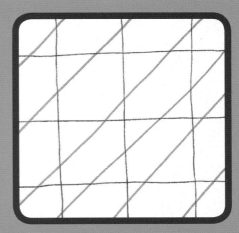

3. Now draw diagonal lines across the grid. Make sure that these lines do not cross the points where the horizontal and vertical lines meet.

4. Fill in all the triangles with your pen to make a pattern of stretched star shapes.

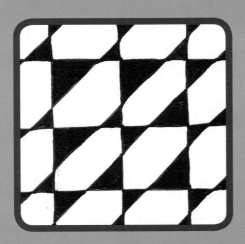

5. Your tangle is complete!

Tangle Tip!
Try to keep your diagonal lines as straight as possible, to make your tangle really pop!

Flower Fairy

Work your magic on this pretty fairy dressed in petals and fill your picture with flowery tangles.

1. Draw a pretty flower fairy holding a flower. Add layers of petals to the dress to fill with different tangles.

2. Choose your tangles and begin to fill the sections. I've used Tipple for the middle of the flower and Daviso for the petals.

3. For the dress, I used Betweed for the sleeve and the top layer of the skirt. The bottom layer is filled with Tortuca and the bodice and shoes are Printemps. Huggins works well for the wings.

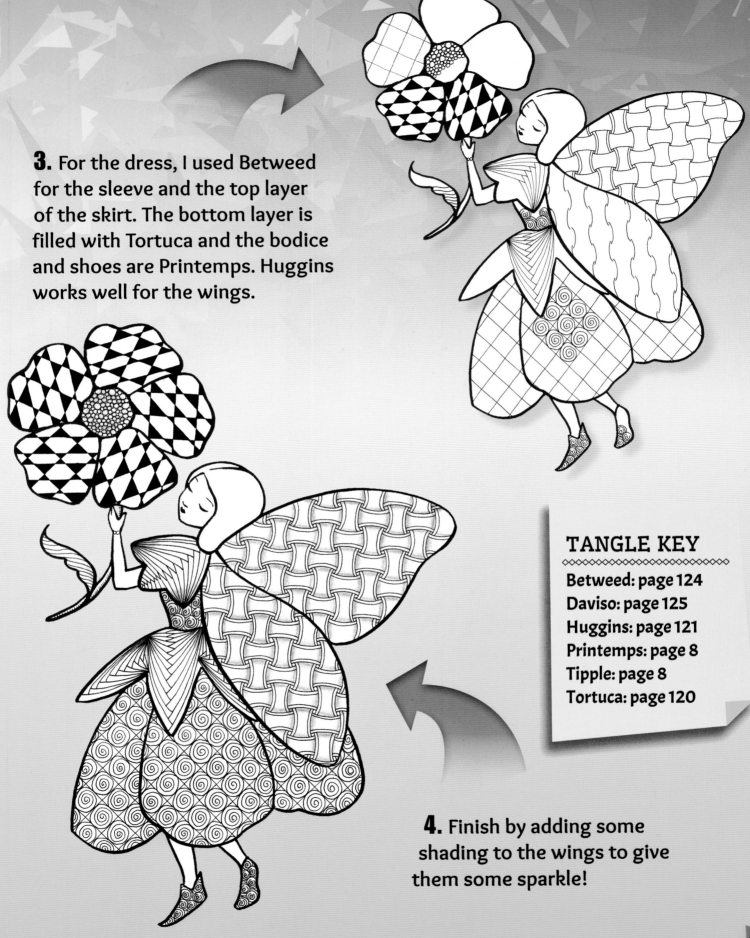

TANGLE KEY

Betweed: page 124
Daviso: page 125
Huggins: page 121
Printemps: page 8
Tipple: page 8
Tortuca: page 120

4. Finish by adding some shading to the wings to give them some sparkle!

Tangle Time!

Use some magical tangles to complete these fantasy characters.